D1546431

PROPERTY OF CEI

Why Regulate Utilities?

Why Regulate Utilities?

The New Institutional Economics and the
Chicago Gas Industry, 1849–1924

Werner Troesken

Ann Arbor
THE UNIVERSITY OF MICHIGAN PRESS

Copyright © by the University of Michigan 1996
All rights reserved
Published in the United States of America by
The University of Michigan Press
Manufactured in the United States of America
⊗ Printed on acid-free paper

1999   1998   1997   1996   4   3   2   1

No part of this publication may be reproduced, stored in a retrieval system, or transmitted in any form or by any means, electronic, mechanical, or otherwise without the written permission of the publisher.

A CIP catalog record for this book is available from the British Library

Library of Congress Cataloging-in-Publication Data

Troesken, Werner, 1963–
    Why regulate utilities? : the new institutional economics and the
Chicago gas industry, 1849–1924 / Werner Troesken.
        p.   cm.
    Includes bibliographical references and index.
    ISBN 0-472-10739-9
    1. Gas industry—Government policy—Illinois—Chicago—History.
2. Gas—Law and legislation—United States—History.   3. Antitrust
law—United States—History.   I. Title.
HD9581.U52C48   1996
363.6'3'0977311—dc20   96-10150
                                                                      CIP

For Patty

Preface

The title of this book refers to Harold Demsetz's classic article, "Why Regulate Utilities?" In the text, I frequently refer as well to Victor Goldberg, Douglass North, and Oliver Williamson. These references suggest the book's audience and arguments. I address primarily economists and historical economists interested in regulation and institutional change. However, I also hope to engage the interests of noneconomists. The book revolves around three arguments. First, building on North, I argue that state utility regulation grew out of a gradual process of institutional change. To fully understand the origins and ends of utility regulation, one needs to probe this larger process of change. Second, building on Williamson, I argue that capital immobility dictated that change be legal and political. Durable and immobile capital bound consumers, gas companies, and local politicians together. When dissatisfied, no group could pursue that common market response—exit. Instead, they had to resolve their disputes through the courts and the legislature. Third, building on Goldberg, I argue that state utility regulation, for all its flaws, was a prudent way to resolve disputes.

Acknowledgments

I thank the many people who commented on my earlier papers. For their detailed comments on the book manuscript itself, I thank Paula Baker, Patty Beeson, Pete Karsten, John Murray, Mark Perlman, and Joel Tarr. I am especially grateful to Andy Rutten for all of his generous help. I owe Douglass North my largest intellectual debt.

Parts of this book are based on two of my previously published papers: "Antitrust Regulation before the Sherman Act: The Break-up of the Chicago Gas Trust Company," *Explorations in Economic History* 32(1): 109–36, reprinted by permission of Academic Press; and "The Institutional Antecedents of State Utility Regulation: The Chicago Gas Industry, 1860–1913," in *The Regulated Economy: A Historical Approach to Political Economy,* edited by Claudia Goldin and Gary Libecap (Chicago: University of Chicago Press). (© 1994 by the National Bureau of Economic Research. All rights reserved.)

Contents

Tables

Figures

Part 1: Theory

CHAPTER 1

The Puzzle of Public Utility Regulation:
An Introduction

Utilities were not always regulated by state commissions. Throughout the nineteenth century, Massachusetts was the only state with a utility commission, and even there the commission had only limited authority. At the same time, state constitutions often forbade local governments from directly regulating rates. It was not until the second decade of the twentieth century that alternative forms of municipal control gave way to state regulation. Between 1907 and 1922, nearly thirty states created utility commissions.[1]

The Origins of Utility Regulation: Three Economic Theories

Utilities were natural monopolies; a single firm could service a market at lower cost than multiple firms. For example, two competing gas companies would have installed two sets of mains when only one set was required. Many economists claim that, in this context, unfettered markets did not work very well. In the short run, competition led to wasteful duplication of capital and brief price wars. In the long run, competing firms merged, consumer prices rose, and the excess capital remained. As the term *natural monopoly* suggests, monopoly was inevitable. Genuine competition was a fleeting and costly hoax.[2]

According to the traditional public interest interpretation of utility regulation, lawmakers created state utility commissions to solve the natural monopoly problem. State commissions prevented wasteful duplication by restricting market entry. They protected consumers against producers' monopoly power by regulating rates. This interpretation suggests that the state acted as an agent for consumers. The state brought consumers an efficient, well-functioning utility system where the market had failed.

The Chicago school interpretation turns the natural monopoly story on its head. As the Chicago story goes, the problem was not that the market failed. On the contrary, the market worked all too well; utilities lobbied for state regulation because they believed it would undermine the market and promote monopoly. In a classic article, Harold Demsetz (1968) writes: "The presence of active rivalry is clearly indicated in public utility history. In fact, producing competitors . . . were so plentiful that one begins to doubt that scale economies characterized the utility industry." From this, Demsetz concludes that

> In the case of utility industries, resort to the rivalry of the market place would relieve companies of the discomforts of commission regulation. But it would also relieve them of the comfort of legally protected market areas. It is my belief that the rivalry of the open market place disciplines more effectively than do the regulatory processes of the commission. If the management of utility companies doubt this belief, I suggest that they re-examine the history of their industry to discover just who it was that provided most of the force behind the regulatory movement.

The Chicago school interpretation suggests that the state acted as an agent for producers. The state brought producers substantial market power where the market had failed.[3]

Recently, a third explanation for the creation of state utility commissions has emerged. Building on the work of Victor Goldberg and Oliver Williamson, this explanation considers the problems of long-term or relational contracting.[4] The following example highlights the underlying logic. To sell gas, a gas company had to invest substantial resources in a system of mains. The investment was irrevocable. Once the mains were in the ground, the gas company could not move or sell them. Strictly speaking, the mains represented an asset specific or non-redeployable investment. If after the company installed its mains, the city imposed onerous price regulations or taxes, the company was stuck. It could not move or resell its capital. As a result, before installing its mains, the gas company required assurances that the city would not impose onerous regulations or taxes ex post. Alternatively, municipal authorities had to grant the gas company the right to use public roads to lay mains. For the city, this right represented an irrevocable investment. Once the gas company exercised its right to use public property and install its mains, the city could not meaningfully revoke that right. If the company's rates or service failed to satisfy the city, the city was stuck.[5] As a result, before granting this property right, the city demanded a commitment that the utility would not charge excessive rates or provide poor service ex post.

According to the relational contracting interpretation, utility industries were never organized as markets, for the same reason that firms are not organized as markets: positive transaction costs (Coase [1937] 1988). Non-redeployable investments forced utilities and municipalities to create long-term, binding contracts. Before state utility regulation, state charters and municipal franchises embodied these contracts and supplanted the market. The charter and franchise governed the behavior of both the municipality and the utility. The state charter set strict limits on the city's regulatory authority. The municipal franchise dictated the price and quality of the company's gas. State utility commissions functioned similarly. Like state charters, they prevented the city from imposing onerous regulations. Like municipal franchises, they prevented the gas company from charging high rates. Hence, the arrival of state regulation represented more of a change in the way cities and utilities contracted than a move from pure and unfettered competition to widespread state intervention.[6]

The policy implications of the public interest and Chicago school interpretations are straightforward. The public interest interpretation implies state regulation should continue. The Chicago school interpretation implies state regulation should cease; control over public utilities should be returned to the market. The Chicago interpretation of utility regulation constitutes a powerful critique of economic regulation in general. Economists have long believed that utilities provided the quintessential example of market failure: namely, natural monopoly. If regulation failed to improve things in markets that were natural monopolies, it would surely fail in situations where claims of market failure were more tenuous.[7] The policy implications of the relational contracting interpretation are less clear and less dramatic. This interpretation suggests that there are a range of possible solutions to the contracting problems that faced utilities and municipalities. State commissions and local franchise agreements offered two alternative solutions. Which solution worked better is not obvious, a priori.

A Historical Critique of the Theories of Utility Regulation

To varying degrees, each of these interpretations explains a part of the history of utility regulation. With its emphasis on natural monopoly, the public interest interpretation explains the highly concentrated market structures observed in utility markets. Throughout the late nineteenth and early twentieth centuries, a single firm dominated gas markets in most towns. Of the 714 towns the 1890 census identifies as having gas service, only 16 had two or more gas companies; of the 827 towns the 1900 census identifies, only 29 had two or more gas companies. With its emphasis on the lobbying efforts of producers, the Chicago school interpretation captures a critical piece of the politics behind utility regulation. Several independent studies reveal that utilities lobbied for state regulation.[8] With its emphasis on asset-specific investments, the relational contracting interpretation explains the presence of municipal franchises and other institutions unique to utility industries.

To varying degrees, each of these interpretations is incomplete. Focusing on natural monopoly, the public interest interpretation cannot account for the unique regulatory experience of utilities, the timing of regulatory change, or the politics behind regulation. First, declining average costs (natural monopoly) did not always induce regulation. After estimating production functions across several industries, John James (1983, 445) writes: "Evaluated relative to the national market, distilling, flour and meal, and pig iron would have been natural monopolies in 1890." Yet none of these industries became regulated by state commissions. Second, lawmakers created nearly all state utility commissions during the fifteen years following 1907. As George Priest (1993, 296) writes, "it is very hard to believe that the average cost curves of gas and electric utilities only began to slope downward after 1907." Finally, the public interest view assumes that lawmakers created utility commissions in response to the demands of consumers. The assumption runs counter to established historical fact. Utilities, not consumers, lobbied for state utility regulation.[9]

Focusing on the politicking of utilities, the Chicago school leaves three unanswered questions. First, if it were merely the lobbying efforts of producers that led to state utility regulation, why were utilities so much more successful than producers in other industries in securing regulation? Surely producers in other industries wanted monopoly profits just as much as utilities. As Herbert Hovenkamp (1991, 6) argues, pressure group politics alone cannot "explain why toll bridges and gaslight utilities in the nineteenth century succeeded so often in acquiring legal monopoly status, while ordinary manufacturers and retailers did not." The timing of regulatory change prompts a second question: if state regulation granted utilities a sure road to monopoly profits, why did utilities wait over half a century to lobby for it? Surely utilities in 1860 desired monopoly profits as much as utilities in 1910. Third, the Chicago school interpretation maintains that municipal authorities were more sympathetic to consumer interests than authorities at the state level. As Gregg Jarrell (1978, 295) writes: "state regulation apparently served to isolate private utilities from the competitive policies of municipal regulators." Why were state regulators more likely to bow to the desires of utilities than municipal regulators?

Focusing on non-redeployable investments, the relational contracting interpretation leaves other issues unresolved. First, without a model of politics, the relational contracting approach cannot account for the lobbying activities of utilities and other interest groups, nor can it account for the different regulatory policies of state and local regulators. Also, without a model of institutional change, the approach cannot explain why one form of credible commitment—state regulatory commissions—eventually replaced another form of commitment—the combination of local franchises and state charters.

Filling the gap between history and theory proves difficult. Aggregating, in whole, the individual theories of utility regulation yields an incoherent picture. How does one combine, in toto, the public interest and Chicago school interpretations? They seem diametrically opposed. The public interest story claims the market failed; the Chicago school claims the market worked well. The public interest story claims regulation curtailed monopoly rates; the Chicago school claims regulation promoted them. A more careful, ad hoc eclecticism is also problematic because all of the theories share a common shortcoming: they cannot account for the dynamics of institutional change. Why, for example, were so many commissions created during the early twentieth century? Simply combining individual pieces of the theories does not provide a complete answer to this and other questions of institutional change.

The Origins of Utility Regulation: A Historical Puzzle

Think of history as a puzzle. To complete the puzzle, we need all of the pieces—we need to know all of the relevant facts. We also need to know how all the pieces fit together—we need a theory to interpret the facts. At present, we can combine pieces here and there: the Chicago school interpretation explains some politics; the natural monopoly interpretation explains something about market structure. But because we have yet to find many pieces in between, the completed fragments of the puzzle are disconnected. Because we have yet to find all the facts, we cannot combine the politics of the Chicago school with the economics of the natural monopoly interpretation. Moreover, once we find the pieces in between, we need to figure out how to combine them. Once we find all of the facts, we need to construct a framework to interpret them.

Analyzing the history of the Chicago gas industry, this book finds some of the puzzle's missing pieces. Borrowing insights from the new institutional economics, it combines these pieces.[10] Two historical contingencies motivate this case study approach. First, the relationships that produced state utility regulation were subtle. With the tightly focused perspective of a case study, one can see these subtleties. With a widely focused perspective, one could easily look past them. Second, the relationships that produced state utility regulation were dynamic. By looking closely at a single industry over time, one gets a deep sense of the forces that animated change as well as the consequences of change.

Briefly stated, here is how the pieces found in Chicago look once they are put together. Chicago gas producers and the city had to make substantial and irrevocable investments in mains and property rights. Initially, producers and the city devised the contractual and institutional arrangements necessary to promote investment in gas mains and property rights. Competitive forces and municipal franchise contracts limited gas producers' ability to charge high rates and provide poor service. Because these institutions prevented gas producers from behaving like a monopolist, city authorities felt comfortable granting them the rights to use the streets to lay mains. Similarly, the Illinois Constitution prevented the Chicago City Council from unilaterally dictating gas rates. Because the state constitution limited the city's regulatory power, producers were confident that they would not be subject to arbitrary or confiscatory rate regulation and felt safe investing in a system of gas mains.

Once the gas mains were installed, both producers and city authorities faced strong incentives to abrogate the institutions that constrained them. Gas companies could make more money if they broke free of the franchises requiring that they charge reasonable rates. Local politicians could extort bribes from gas companies if they broke free of the constitutional rules prohibiting them from regulating rates. Gas companies and local politicians responded to these incentives. They lobbied; they litigated; they used any means possible to abrogate their original commitments. Out of the subsequent legal and political battles, a state regulatory commission emerged.

CHAPTER 2

Solving the Puzzle of Public Utility Regulation: A Framework

In this chapter, I construct a framework to explain why a state commission came to regulate Chicago gas companies. The framework centers on two observations. First, as Goldberg and Williamson suggest, non-redeployable investments pervaded the gas industry. Producers invested in gas mains; city authorities invested in property rights. Second, the institutions that governed the Chicago gas industry evolved over time. During the nineteenth century, Chicago authorities had no power to regulate rates. By 1905, they did. During the nineteenth century, the market worked; new firms entered and drove down prices. By 1900, entry and competition had ceased.

Non-Redeployable Investment: Documentation

In 1890, Chicago produced more goods and services than any other city in the nation, except New York. It poured more iron and steel than any other city except Pittsburgh. It cut more brick, masonry and stone than any other city except Philadelphia. It forged more dies, metals, and tools and slaughtered and packed more meat than any other city. A city that produced so much required capital—lots of capital. The eleventh census states that in 1890, the aggregate amount of physical capital—buildings, machines, railroad track, tools, and so on—owned by Chicago businesses exceeded $350 million. Chicago gas companies owned more than 10 percent of the city's physical capital; the eleventh census states that their investments in gas mains, plants, and other equipment totaled more than $40 million. The only Chicago producers who came close to having this much capital were the meatpackers and slaughterhouses. They owned more than $38 million in physical capital. Chicago's infamous stockyards were, by themselves, a small town.[1]

In 1890, New York was the only city in the nation that produced more goods and services than Chicago. In 1890, the aggregate amount of physical capital owned by New York businesses exceeded $426 million. New

York gas companies owned more than 10 percent of the city's physical capital, more than any other industry in the city.[2]

Forty million dollars. Ten percent of all the buildings, machines, tools, and other capital in Chicago. That was a lot of capital. Gas companies put most of it in the ground. By 1906, Chicago gas companies had laid over two thousand miles of mains. According to one official, it would have taken "10,000 to 15,000 men, working constantly, summer and winter, two years to lay 2,000 miles of mains." Other sources suggest that during the early 1890s it cost about $135,000, in 1991 dollars, to lay one mile of gas mains. Once in the ground, mains lasted about fifty years. In Chicago, however, an unusually damp soil shortened main life.[3]

Why did gas mains cost so much? Mains were made of cast iron. Engineers advised that they measure more than four inches in diameter and weigh no less than 220 pounds per twelve-foot length of pipe. Large high-pressure mains, those more than twenty inches in diameter, weighed over a ton. Given the size and weight of mains, laborers worked in groups while installing them. In large cities, main gangs typically consisted of twenty-five workers. In Chicago, workers placed mains thirty inches or more below ground to reduce the stress caused by cold weather and heavy traffic. Workers also pitched the mains, angling them downward at a rate of less than one inch per one hundred feet. Pitching prevented sulfur and tar residuals from building up and clogging the main. As coal gas traveled through the main, elements of sulfur and tar separated from the gas and settled on the bottom of the main. The tar and sulfur flowed to a drip box. Periodically, workers drained the drip box with a pump. In central sections of the city, a drip box was placed at every intersection. Bell and spigot joints linked individual lengths of pipe. Caulking the joints with soft lead and jute (a burlaplike yarn) kept the joints from leaking. Placing blocks of wood underneath the mains prevented settlement. Settlement caused joints to break open. Even trench excavation and backfilling required care. After digging the trench, workers separated the earth, stone, and gravel into piles. In backfilling, workers returned large stones first, tamped them into place, returned the smaller stones second, tamped them into place, and so on, until they reached the top soil. Sloppy backfill settled, causing streets to buckle and dip.[4]

Manufacturing coal gas required smaller, more mobile investments than did distributing coal gas. A gas plant large enough to service Chicago cost about 10 percent of the cost of installing five hundred miles of mains. Gas plants usually lasted between twenty-five and thirty-three years. Briefly, producers manufactured coal gas by filling a series of clay boxes with several tons of coal. Heating the coal to a temperature of 1,000 to

2,500 degrees Fahrenheit for five to sixty hours distilled the gas. (Appendix A describes the technology of gas production in greater detail.)[5]

Non-Redeployable Investment and Political Opportunism

There were degrees of non-redeployability. Some businesses, like small retailers, could have easily moved or resold their capital. Small retailers who wanted to exit the Chicago market, or leave the retail business altogether, needed only to let their leases expire or sell their store space to other businesses. Whatever inventories they possessed they could have also easily moved or resold.

Some businesses, like steel mills and slaughterhouses, found it more difficult to move or resell their capital. If mills and slaughterhouses wanted to exit the Chicago market by selling their steel and meat in other cities, that was easy enough. They put the steel on a barge and the meat in a refrigerated railcar. Physically relocating their plant and capital was harder, but possible. They could have scrapped and sold their factory buildings, their land, and some of their machinery. The only problem was that all this capital would have been customized to the idiosyncratic needs of the steel mills and slaughterhouses. Consequently, mills and slaughterhouses would have recovered only a fraction of their original investments.

Some businesses, like gas companies, found it impossible to move or resell their capital. The technology of distribution locked gas companies into the Chicago market. Because of the enormous costs of installing mains, gas companies could not easily exploit markets in other cities. Unlike steel mills and slaughterhouses, they could not just put their product on a barge or railroad car. Moreover, because gas mains had no other uses, gas producers faced a very thin secondary market. Steel mills and slaughterhouses could have scrapped their buildings and machines and sold them, at a discount, for other industrial uses. Gas companies could not have sold mains for anything except distributing gas. Chicago, therefore, held the gas mains hostage. Producers could not have moved to another market without sacrificing them.

Non-redeployable capital increased the risks of investing in the gas industry. Suppose consumers captured the city's regulatory apparatus and secured passage of an ordinance requiring gas companies to charge very low rates. Because gas mains locked producers into the Chicago market, they could not have avoided the regulation by exiting and selling to consumers elsewhere. In contrast, suppose the city passed an ordinance requiring a very low price on all meat sold in the city. Meatpackers simply would have shipped their products to other geographic markets to avoid the regulation. Unlike gas companies, they did not need to move their capital to exploit other markets. If the proconsumer spin on this example seems contrived, assume instead that the city council used the threat of low rates to extort bribes from the gas companies: "pay us off or we'll let you have it."

I do not imply that all attempts to regulate gas rates were opportunistic. Protecting consumers against producers' market power was a legitimate and worthy goal. I only suggest that capital immobility left producers vulnerable to the whims of local politicians. As my discussion in chapter 6 makes clear, sometimes local politicians found it expedient to push a worthy goal beyond reasonable limits.

The Institutional Foundations of
Non-Redeployable Investment

Before investing, Chicago gas companies needed assurances that once they installed their mains city authorities would not impose onerous regulations. During the nineteenth century, four institutions—the Illinois Constitution, the U.S. Constitution, the city's reputation, and state charters—constrained the regulatory power of the Chicago City Council. These four institutions gave producers the guarantees they needed to feel safe investing in the gas industry. First, the Illinois Constitution forbade municipal governments from regulating utility rates. If local authorities tried to set rates, onerous or otherwise, the courts would not have allowed it. (Chapters 4 and 5 discuss this constitutional provision in detail.)

Second, the principle of substantive due process protected utilities against confiscatory rate regulation. One early commentator explains: "If the legislature . . . fixes rates which are so low as to be non-compensatory, there is a confiscation which deprives the utility of its property without due process of law." The courts first articulated this rule in the *Reagan* cases in 1894 and in *Smyth v. Ames* in 1897. When utilities sued for Fourteenth Amendment protection, the courts granted immediate injunctive relief only in cases where the evidence clearly showed that regulators had set confiscatory rates. In ambiguous cases, the courts allowed the rates to go into effect. If the company met its financial obligations, the rates were remunerative and remained. If not, the rates were confiscatory and were enjoined.[6]

Third, the city's desire to encourage future investment may have prevented it from actively promoting low rates when gas producers first began investing in the city. If the city forced gas producers to charge low rates throughout the 1850s, gas producers, as well as other utilities, would have been reluctant to invest during the 1860s. The city, however, confronted an endgame problem. Once utilities neared completion of their networks, the city's incentive to encourage future investment fell.

Finally, for part of the nineteenth century, state charters helped promote investment. The charters granted to Chicago gas producers set strict limits on the regulatory power of the city and, initially, gave producers exclusive control over the city's gas market. While chapter 3 discusses these charters in detail, for now, two observations are relevant. First, by enabling gas producers to recoup their investments up front, grants of monopoly power functioned as a form of credible commitment. Crudely, if because of their monopoly privileges gas producers recouped their investment within ten years, who would have cared how regulators behaved during the next twenty years? Second, a charter was a contract between the state and the gas company. The state could not unilaterally alter it.

On the second point, the case of *Louisville Gas Co. v. Citizens' Gas-Light Co.* is instructive. In January 1869, the Kentucky legislature granted the Louisville Gas Company a charter. The charter gave the company the exclusive privilege of providing Louisville with gas for twenty years. In 1872, the state incorporated the Citizens' Gas-Light Company, giving it the authority to manufacture and distribute gas in Louisville. A few years later, the Citizens' Company sued. The company asked that the court perpetually enjoin the Louisville Gas Company from exercising the exclusive right to manufacture and sell gas in the city. The United States Supreme Court denied the injunction and upheld the Louisville Company's right to exclusivity. The court explained that the Louisville Company's charter, which promised the company an exclusive market, was a contract between the state and the company. By subsequently granting a charter to the Citizens' Company, the Kentucky legislature impaired the obligation of that contract. In as much as the U.S. Constitution forbade legislation impairing the obligation of contract, the charter of the Citizens' Company was void.[7]

How the City Protected Itself

As I noted earlier, city authorities, like gas companies, had to make irrevocable investments. Once the city gave a gas company the right to use the streets, it soon became impossible to revoke that right. Consumers also had to make irrevocable investments to use gas. In the twentieth century, consumers purchased gas stoves and furnaces. In the nineteenth century, consumers purchased gaslighting fixtures. These fixtures were often immobile and had no alternative use. To get the rights needed to lay mains and to induce consumers to purchase the necessary fixtures, gas producers needed to commit themselves to competitive rates and good service.

Two institutions limited producers' ability to behave opportunistically. First, competitive forces limited gas producers' market power. Between 1880 and 1900, ten new gas companies organized in Chicago. Real gas prices were halved. However, as the next chapter makes clear, one can easily overstate the efficacy of market forces. Second, through municipal franchises, the city granted gas companies the rights they needed to lay and repair mains. In return for these rights, gas companies agreed to charge low rates and to provide gas of a specified quality. Also, gas companies sometimes agreed to pay the city a percentage of their earnings. Presumably this compensated the city for the costs it incurred while the gas companies dug up the streets. It is not clear, however, if gas companies paid full compensation. By the late nineteenth century, some groups in Chicago lamented the low taxes paid by gas and other utilities. As state charters constituted a contract between state authorities and gas companies, municipal franchises constituted a contract between local authorities and gas companies. If the gas company tried to charge a rate higher than that set by the franchise, the city or individual consumers could sue for damages or an injunction. Gas companies sometimes tried to work around rate ceilings by charging a meter rent or by adding other fixed charges to customers' bills. The courts took a dim view of such actions.[8]

Municipal franchises sometimes expressed price ceilings in nominal dollars. Nominal price ceilings worked poorly. Between 1865 and 1890, the general price level fell steadily (see fig. 1). As the price of most goods and services fell, nominal rate ceilings remained the same; real rate ceilings rose. Consequently, nominal rate ceilings often failed to bind gas companies after a few years. For example, Cleveland issued a franchise to the Peoples Gas Light Company in 1867. The franchise prohibited the company from charging more than $3 per one thousand cubic feet (MCF). By the early 1870s, Peoples Gas charged $2.[9]

Some local governments tied rate ceilings to gas prices in similar cities. Others reserved the right to regulate rates in the future. In Saginaw, Michigan, the gas company's franchise prohibited rates higher than the average price in "cities of like population." Through the franchise, the Saginaw City Council also reserved the right to regulate rates after five years. The franchise stipulated, however, that the council could not reduce rates below those in "similarly situated" cities. In Minneapolis, Minnesota, the gas company's franchise prohibited rates from "exceeding those charged by companies in neighboring cities, regard being had to freight and charges for material for manufacturing gas."[10]

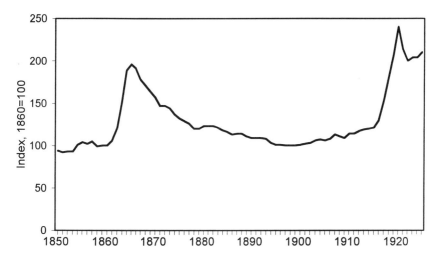

Fig. 1. Consumer price index, 1850–1925. (From McCusker [1992], 328–30, table A-2, column 6, Composite Consumer Price Index.)

A Model of Institutional Change

Many of the institutions I described previously—the state charters, the local franchises, the state constitution, and so on—evolved over time. As institutions evolved, so did the ability of producers and city authorities to behave opportunistically. In 1897, producers secured passage of a law inhibiting entry into the gas industry. The law undermined the market mechanism, an institution that had once prevented gas companies from charging monopoly rates. In 1905, the Illinois legislature passed a law empowering the Chicago City Council to regulate gas rates. The law undermined the state constitution, an institution that had once prevented the city from imposing onerous regulations. Understanding why these and other legal changes occurred and why they eventually led to the creation of a state utilities commission requires a theory of institutional change.

Douglass North (1990) builds such a theory. There are two key elements in North's theory of change: organizations and institutions. Organizations are groups of people bound by common goals. Institutions are the rules that govern and constrain human behavior. North classifies institutions as formal and informal. Informal institutions refer to cultural norms and codes of conduct. Formal institutions refer to legally enforceable contracts and the laws promulgated by judges and legislators. I focus on formal institutions.

Institutions influence the organizing process in two ways. First, institutions determine society's incentive structure; they tell people what it pays to organize for. Second, institutions, along with more traditional economic constraints like income and time, act as behavioral constraints; they tell people what types of organizations and goals are feasible. Organizations are not only a response to institutions, they are also a source of institutional change. While achieving their objectives, organizations try to alter, to their own favor, the laws and contracts that control them. In this way, North's organizations earn profits not only through the traditional avenues considered by economists—innovation, adoption of efficient production and management technologies, collusion, and so on—but also through rent-seeking, that is, by using the political process to transfer resources away from other groups to themselves (North 1990, 4–8).

Institutional change results when the (perceived) benefits of change exceed the costs. Alternatively, stability results when the costs of change exceed the benefits. Stability does not imply that everyone is content. It only means that no group or person finds it profitable to alter the prevailing institutional framework (North 1990, 86).

Shocks to population, preferences, and technology cause relative price changes. Relative price changes cause institutional change whenever they are large enough to make it profitable for some organization to alter the prevailing legal and regulatory framework. Institutional change, however, is itself a source of relative price changes. By altering relative prices, an initial institutional change may increase the benefits of additional legal change, inducing some organization to secure that secondary change. This, in turn, may make further institutional changes profitable, and so on. In short, institutions can evolve in a wavelike pattern, with a single change begetting further changes (North 1990, 83–84, 86).

To illustrate, consider the origins of federal antitrust legislation. During the late nineteenth century, technological changes increased scale economies in many industries (James 1983). As scale economies grew, so did the benefits of merger and consolidation. Business organizations responded; the number of trusts and other industrial combinations proliferated (Chandler 1977). The trust movement, itself an institutional change, altered relative prices. The price changes hurt several groups. The meatpacking trust reduced meat prices, driving small butchers out of business (Libecap 1992). Standard Oil reduced oil prices, driving small oil refiners out of business (Troesken 1994). The jute-bagging trust increased the price of jute bags to cotton farmers (McMath 1975). These groups, and others displaced by the trust movement, responded by lobbying for a federal antitrust statute. The Sherman Antitrust Act followed.

The antitrust act, and its subsequent enforcement, induced further institutional changes. Alfred Chandler (1977, 333) argues that because of the judiciary's interpretation of the Sherman Act, "lawyers were advising their corporate clients to abandon all agreements or alliances carried out through cartels or trade associations and to consolidate into single, legally defined enterprises." The act not only encouraged producers to alter their modes of combination, it also drove them to secure additional legislative changes. Gabriel Kolko (1963, 259) writes: "the business community resented the insecurity of the Sherman Act and wished to attain a measure of predictability and confidence that had been lacking." A desire to amend the Sherman Act drove business to lobby for the Hepburn Bill of 1908, the Clayton Act, and the Federal Trade Commission Act (Kolko 1963, 132–35, 253–70).

Non-Redeployable Investment and Institutional Change in Chicago

Utility regulation in Chicago evolved in much the same way as federal antitrust policy; in Chicago, as with federal antitrust policy, a technological change set in motion waves of institutional change. I divide Chicago's narrative into five periods: an early period of stability; a more dynamic competitive period; a period of unregulated monopoly; a period of municipal-regulated monopoly; and a final, stable period of state-regulated monopoly. From the Chicago gas industry's inception in 1850 through 1880, two companies dominated the city's gas market. Through a restrictive covenant, the companies divided the city into separate and exclusive market shares. In 1878, an exogenous technology shock brought an end to this period of stability. Within a decade, six new gas companies entered the industry, and real gas prices fell by over 50 percent. Gas companies tried to suppress the new competition, first by organizing a holding company and then, later, by organizing a trust. Chicago consumers and politicians countered these efforts, sponsoring a series of antitrust suits against producers.

Eventually, continued market entry and antitrust prosecution drove gas producers to lobby the state legislature for relief. Because of producers' lobbying, in 1897 the Illinois legislature passed the gas acts. Fully explained in chapter 5, the gas acts inhibited market entry and removed the common law obstacles to merger and consolidation. After the passage of these laws, no new firms entered the Chicago gas industry. Incumbent firms merged into a single firm. Gas rates rose. The gas acts initiated Chicago's third phase, unregulated monopoly. Consumers, civic reform groups, and local politicians organized in response to the gas acts. They sponsored legal suits to have the laws declared unconstitutional, they petitioned for injunctions preventing gas companies from increasing prices, and they had the city council pass ordinances ordering gas companies to reduce rates. Although these efforts failed, the lobbying efforts of local politicians and reform groups eventually led the state legislature to pass the Enabling Act of 1905. The Enabling Act granted the Chicago City Council the authority to regulate gas rates in the city. The act initiated Chicago's fourth phase, municipal-regulated monopoly.

Claiming that municipal regulation was arbitrary and confiscatory, producers worked to undermine the Enabling Act. They first tried to forestall municipal rate regulation through the courts. They also supported the creation of a state utilities commission. Although Chicago gas companies generally preferred as little regulatory interference as possible, they saw state regulation as one way to prevent the hostile policies of municipal authorities. The lobbying efforts of Chicago gas companies encouraged the state legislature to create a state utilities commission in 1913. Unlike earlier regulatory regimes, state regulation was stable, and a state commission still regulates Illinois utilities today.

In light of North's model, four aspects of Chicago's narrative stand out. First, organizations were the agents of institutional change. Producers' lobbying efforts led to passage of the gas acts and the creation of a state regulatory commission; consumers' lobbying efforts led to passage of the Enabling Act and several antitrust suits against producers. Second, relative price changes motivated the efforts of different groups to secure institutional change. After technological changes caused gas rates in Chicago to plummet, gas producers adopted new institutional arrangements—for example, creating a holding company and a trust—to prevent further rate reductions. After the gas acts, and the associated increase in consumer gas prices, consumers organized and lobbied for the Enabling Act to prevent further rate increases. Third, as in the discussion of antitrust legislation, state regulation grew out of a wavelike process of institutional change; increased competition gave rise to the gas acts; the gas acts gave rise to the Enabling Act; and the Enabling Act gave rise to a state utilities commission. Fourth, the relative price changes that followed state regulation were not large enough to generate further institutional change. State regulation was an institutional equilibrium.

In Chicago, capital immobility determined the path of institutional change. Consider the city's experience with municipal rate regulation. Recall that gas companies found municipal regulation arbitrary and confiscatory. If capital had been mobile, overzealous rate regulation would have driven gas companies out of the city and constrained the regulatory efforts of municipal authorities. Remember the earlier example of meatpackers and steel mills; if the city imposed price ceilings on their products, they would have sold them elsewhere. However, because gas producers could not move or sell their mains, they were forced to seek protection against municipal regulators through the courts and the state legislature. In short, because capital was immobile, politically administered solutions, such as a state regulatory commission, as opposed to market-administered solutions, such as exit, became more likely.

Non-Redeployable Investment and Models of Politics

In Chicago, gas consumers were an important political force. Their political activity poses a conundrum. The standard theory of collective action suggests that consumers would have been politically innocuous.[11] As an illustration, consider why the standard logic predicts tariffs instead of free trade. A tariff places a tax on imports. The tax benefits domestic producers by insulating them against foreign competition. The tax hurts consumers because it raises the price of imported goods as well as domestically produced goods—by shielding domestic producers against foreign competition, the tariff gives domestic firms greater freedom to raise their prices. Because producers are usually few, the benefits of the tariff are spread across a small group. Because consumers are many, the costs of the tariff are spread across a large group. Producers thus face strong incentives to lobby for the tariff while consumers face a small incentive to lobby against the tariff. A tariff on Toyotas earns GM many more dollars than it costs the typical car buyer. Beyond this, because producers are few and geographically concentrated in comparison to consumers, it is easier for them to organize for collective action. The Big Three are all in Detroit; car buyers are distributed across the country. In short, for producers the benefits of organizing and lobbying for tariffs are high while the costs are low. For consumers, the benefits of organizing and lobbying against tariffs are low while the costs are high.

In the gas industry, however, geographic-specific capital mitigated these free-rider problems. Compare, for example, the ability of the consumers of dressed beef to organize an effective lobbying force against the ability of gas consumers to organize. Although most dressed-beef companies were located in Chicago, they shipped their beef, by refrigerated rail cars, to consumers across the nation. In contrast, the technology of gas distribution meant that Chicago gas companies sold only to customers in the Chicago area. Because gas consumers, unlike the consumers of dressed beef and most other products, were concentrated in a single region, it would have been easier for them to overcome the free-rider problems that typically forestall effective consumer action.

Beyond this, even if gas consumers were unable to organize as effectively as producers, their power at the ballot box may have influenced legislative outcomes. Denzau and Munger (1986) show that it is difficult (costly) for an organized interest group to win a legislator's support if voters in the legislator's district are opposed to the policies the interest group promotes. For example, who would the Sierra Club more easily influence, the legislator representing a district where most voters work in the lumber and fishing industries or the legislator representing a district where most voters work in urban environments? Usually, the legislator from the urban district would be more sympathetic to the Sierra Club because the club advocates policies that would reduce employment in lumber and fishing while preserving recreational lands for urban naturalists. This example assumes that voters are well informed and rational. Voters, that is, are assumed to know how their representative votes and to understand the effects of the Sierra Club's policy proposals. If, however, voters lack information or are not rational, it would be easier for the legislator to ignore their preferences.

Denzau and Munger's model suggests that the preferences of unorganized voters may have limited the ability of gas producers to manipulate the political process to their own ends. If voters wanted low gas rates, they would have voted out of office legislators who promoted high rates. Of course, the effectiveness of Chicago voters depended critically on the cost of information and the level of voter rationality. If voters were unaware or did not fully understand the effects of laws like the gas acts, gas producers would have had an easy time accomplishing their agenda. Importantly, the efficacy of voters varied across jurisdictions and levels of government. Compare, for example, the ability of voters to monitor politicians at the state and local levels. Because voters at the municipal level were few and geographically concentrated compared with voters at the state level, the logic of collective action predicts that municipal voters would have monitored municipal politicians better than state voters monitored state politicians. Free-rider problems would have been less severe at the local level. In chapter 7, I develop this idea and use it to explain why Chicago gas producers preferred state regulation to municipal regulation.

I think it would be a mistake to focus solely on the politicking of producers. Instead, I adopt a multiple interest group perspective, one that considers consumers and producers.[12] A multiple interest group perspective has two attractive features. First, it is the first step in reconciling the standard public interest and Chicago school interpretations. It allows for the possibility that both producers and consumers influenced the legislative process. Second, it explains the institutional ebb and flow observed in Chicago. That is, it helps explain how the Illinois legislature could pass proproducer laws (the gas acts) in 1897 and then, a few years later, pass a proconsumer law (the Enabling Act). Simply put, the relative strength of competing interest groups varied over time. In 1897, producers exercised greater influence over the legislature, while a few years later consumers held the upper hand.

The Courts and Institutional Change

In Chicago, litigation was a response to relative price changes. When local regulators lowered rates, gas companies sued for Fourteenth Amendment protection; when gas companies raised rates, consumers and local politicians sought redress through antitrust suits. In Chicago, litigation was also a source of relative price changes. When the courts offered gas companies Fourteenth Amendment protection, they caused gas rates to rise; when the courts busted the gas trust, they at least hoped to reduce rates. As a source of relative price changes, litigation generated additional institutional change. When the courts busted the gas trust, the trust lobbied for the consolidation act, a law that undermined the courts' trust-busting efforts; when the courts disallowed the rates set by city authorities, local authorities lobbied for the Enabling Act, a law that expanded the city's regulatory power. Because interest groups and voters often called on legislators to undo the actions of judges, the ultimate effect of any legal decision cannot be fully understood without considering the decision's larger political context. In other words, the courts were endogenous. They were a part of the process. They were both prompting, and responding to, economic and political change.[13]

Beyond this, at the state level, political forces shaped how the courts responded to change. Unlike federal judges, Illinois judges were elected. As originally set forth in the state constitution, the Illinois Supreme Court consisted of seven justices, each representing a separate and distinct judicial district. Justices were elected to serve nine-year terms. They could also run for reelection. The structure of the circuit and appellate courts was more involved. Because a detailed description of that structure would be distracting here, suffice it to say that appellate and circuit court judges were elected to six-year terms.[14] An elected state judiciary gave Chicago voters another avenue through which they could influence policy. The chapters that follow suggest that it was an important one.

Part 2: History

CHAPTER 3

Competition, 1849–97

Throughout the nineteenth and early twentieth century, people used coal gas to light their homes. Until the late 1870s, lighting gas was a luxury; in 1870, it would have cost more than 15 percent of the average laborer's income to light a Chicago home with gas. Gas companies thus sold primarily to businesses and the wealthy. Competition from other lighting sources, such as kerosene, helped limit the demand for gas; in 1870, it cost more to light a home with gas than with oil lamps. During the late 1870s and early 1880s, technological changes caused large reductions in gas rates. Rate reductions, combined with the fact that gas gave off four times more light than kerosene and was cleaner and safer, helped expand the market for coal gas. By 1900, 9 percent of all families in the United States lit their homes with gas. This was three times the number of families who used electricity. (By 1920, 35 percent of all families lit their homes with gas; about the same number used electricity. By 1940, 21 percent of all families lit their homes with gas; 79 percent used electricity.) Gaslight was an urban phenomenon. In 1899, Chicago, New York, Philadelphia, and St. Louis together consumed half of all coal gas produced. In rural areas, kerosene lamps remained the most common form of lighting until well into the twentieth century.[1]

Competition from electricity and natural gas gradually undermined the market for coal gas. Electricity drove consumers away from the use of gas for light and toward its use for heating and cooking. Electricity was a safer and eventually cheaper lighting source than gas. By 1919, the proportion of coal gas used for purposes of illumination fell to about 20 percent. Because people used coal gas for both heat and light, for a long time it remained more popular than electricity. For example, in Chicago in 1916, there were nearly 655,000 coal gas consumers and only 302,899 electric consumers in the city. However, as electricity eroded the gaslighting market, natural gas eroded the coal gas heating and cooking market. With two times more heat energy per cubic foot than coal gas, natural gas was a superior heating fuel. By the 1960s, residential consumers had stopped using coal gas for either light or heat.[2]

The Early History of the Chicago Coal Gas Industry

In 1849, Illinois chartered Chicago's first gas company, the Chicago Gas Light and Coke Company. The company's charter granted it "the exclusive privilege of supplying the city of Chicago and the inhabitants with gas, for the purpose of affording light for ten years." Because the charter set no limits on price or quality, local consumers and politicians frequently complained about high rates. In 1855, Illinois chartered the Peoples Gas Light and Coke Company. The charter forbade the company from beginning operations until 1859, when the Chicago Gas Light Company's right to exclusivity expired. In 1865, the state amended the charter of the Peoples Gas Light and Coke Company, empowering the Chicago City Council to regulate the company's rates for ten years. The state, however, prohibited the city from reducing rates below $3 per MCF.[3]

The Peoples Gas Light and Coke Company did not begin manufacturing and distributing gas until June 1, 1862. In the same year, Peoples Gas and Chicago Gas entered into a restrictive covenant. They divided Chicago into two exclusive markets and agreed not to compete with one another for one hundred years. The Chicago Gas Light Company enjoyed exclusive control over the city's north and south sides. Peoples Gas enjoyed exclusive control over the city's west side. (There was no east side, just Lake Michigan.) As shown in figure 2, the Chicago Gas Light Company operated east of the Chicago River, south of Irving Park Boulevard, and north of 39th Street. Peoples Gas operated west of the Chicago River, east of Kedzie Avenue, south of Belmont Avenue, and north of 39th Street.

For nearly two decades, neither firm attempted to enter the other's territory. Also, except for the Hyde Park Gas Company, a small suburban concern organized in 1871, no new firms entered the industry.[4]

The Introduction of Water Gas

The commercial introduction of water gas disrupted this period of stability. Water gas became commercially viable during the 1870s.[5] Like ordinary coal gas, producers distilled water gas by heating coals. In distilling water gas, however, producers passed steam and a vaporized oil through the incandescent beds of coal to increase the lighting power of the gas. Appendix A gives a detailed description of water gas technology.

Water gas had three advantages over ordinary coal gas. First, water gas had greater illuminating power. Second, water gas plants incurred about half the labor and repair costs incurred by coal gas plants. Third, water gas reduced the fixed costs of production. The manager of a St.

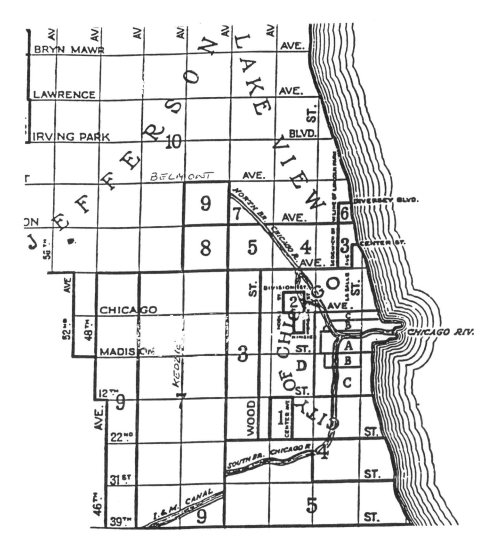

Fig. 2. Chicago street map. (From Pierce [1957], 334.)

Louis gas company claimed that a coal gas plant required "150 percent more investment" than a water gas plant. For "equivalent capacity," a water gas apparatus cost less to install and required much less ground space for fuel and the apparatus itself. Space requirements were so low that in 1889 one industry observer described a water gas plant "completely installed in an old church building 30 × 50 feet."[6]

Because of these advantages, water gas gradually replaced coal gas. In 1875, there were only a handful of water gas plants in the United States. By 1890, there were over 350 plants, producing 40 percent of all gas manufactured in the United States. By 1900, water gas plants manufactured about 75 percent of all gas in the United States.[7]

Older coal gas manufactures tried to suppress water gas. They claimed that it increased the risk of death and injury by asphyxiation. The basis for this claim was that water gas generated high levels of carbonic oxide, a highly toxic and odorless gas. Ostensibly in response to this danger, Massachusetts passed a law prohibiting the distribution of gas "that contain[ed] more than ten percent of carbonic oxide."[8]

Leaking gas, coal or water, was often fatal. Stories of people dying as the result of undetected gas leaks dot nineteenth- and early-twentieth-century newspapers. It is not clear, however, that the dangers of water gas exceeded those associated with ordinary coal gas. The petroleum vapors introduced into water gas diluted the carbonic oxide. They also gave the gas an unpleasant and noticeable odor, making it easier to detect gas leaks. For these reasons, Edward S. Wood, a professor of chemistry at Harvard University, concluded that water gas was "but little if anymore dangerous than common coal gas."[9]

Water Gas and Market Structure in Chicago

By lowering the fixed costs of production, water gas attracted several new firms to the Chicago gas industry. On April 29, 1882, the Chicago City Council granted a perpetual, and nontransferable franchise to the Consumers Gas, Fuel and Light Company. The franchise allowed the company to lay gas mains throughout the city. The franchise also prohibited the company from charging private consumers more than $1.75; in 1882, gas prices in Chicago ranged between $2.25 and $2.50 per MCF. Finally, the franchise prohibited the Consumers Company from combining with other Chicago gas companies. Consumers Gas operated in the north and south divisions of the city, previously the exclusive territory of the Chicago Gas Light and Coke Company.[10]

In 1885, the Equitable Gas Light and Fuel Company organized. The city granted Equitable a franchise nearly identical to that of the Consumers Company. The Peoples Gas Light and Coke Company organized the Equitable Gas Company to operate on the city's south side (Pierce 1957, 222). (Recall that its 1862 contract with the Chicago Gas Light and Coke Company prohibited Peoples Gas from directly entering the north and south sides of the city.)

Other entrants during the 1880s were suburban concerns and/or subsidiaries of larger Chicago gas companies. Organized in 1881, the Lake Gas Company operated solely in the town of Lake. Organized in 1884, the Suburban Gas Company also operated in Lake. It was a subsidiary of the Chicago Gas Light and Coke Company. Organized in 1885, the Calumet Gas Company operated in Hyde Park. Also organized in 1885, the Illinois Light, Heat and Power Company did not distribute gas to residential consumers. It sold most of its output to the Peoples Gas Light and Coke Company.[11]

The introduction of water gas, and the market entry that followed, caused gas prices to fall. On Chicago's north and south sides, a price war erupted. In July of 1883, the Chicago Gas Light and Coke Company lowered its price from $2.25 to $1.75 per MCF to match the price of the Consumers Company. Again, in November, the Chicago Gas Company reduced its price from $1.75 to $1.00. Consumers Gas responded by cutting its price to $1.00. While nominal prices fell by over 50 percent on the north and south sides, they fell by only 25 percent on the city's west side, where the Peoples Gas Light and Coke Company reduced its price from $2.00 to $1.50.

As figure 3 illustrates, these nominal price changes translated into a 50 percent reduction in real gas rates. For the first time, lighting gas became affordable to large segments of the Chicago population. In 1883 alone, the Consumers Gas Company attracted seven thousand to eight thousand new customers to the industry. Between 1883 and 1886, Peoples Gas attracted another 9,627 customers.[12]

Profits fell as prices fell. The price war between the Chicago Gas Light and Coke Company and the Consumers Gas, Fuel and Light Company forced Consumers Gas into bankruptcy. In 1886, the company reorganized under the name Consumers Gas Company. At the same time, the Equitable Gas Light and Fuel Company neared bankruptcy as it "had not yet reached a point where it could earn fixed charges." Finally, between June 1883 and September 1883, the stock price of the Chicago Gas Light and Coke Company fell from 147 1/2 to 100. The reduction coincided with the company's price war with the Consumers Company.[13]

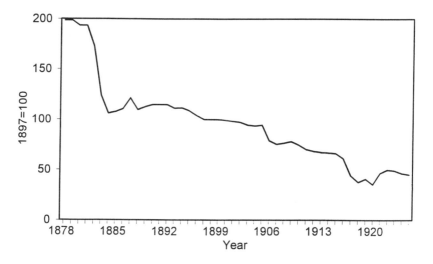

Fig. 3. Index of Chicago gas prices in constant dollars, 1878–1924 (aver-
age of prices on the city's north, south, and west sides). (Data for
Chicago gas prices from Illinois Bureau of Labor Statistics [1897], 278;
Peoples Gas Light and Coke Company [1900]; Bemis [1911], 28; and
Browns Directory of American Gas Companies, vols. 1910–25. Data for
general price level from McCusker [1992], 328–30, table A-2, column 6,
Composite Consumer Price Index.)

The Formation of the Chicago Gas Trust Company

In May 1886, the Chicago Gas Light and Coke Company installed gas
mains on the west side of the city, breaking its one-hundred-year covenant
with the Peoples Gas Light and Coke Company. The Peoples Company
sued, asking the courts to enforce the covenant. The state supreme court,
however, refused to enforce the contract. Writing for the court, Justice
Magruder ruled that "the contract between these two corporations tends
to create and perpetuate a monopoly in the furnishing of gas to the city."
As a result, the court reasoned, the agreement could not be reconciled with
the intentions of the Illinois legislature. When the state legislature chartered the Peoples Gas Light and Coke Company, it intended to promote
competition. The legislature wanted the monopoly in the Chicago gas
industry to cease. The restrictive covenant "sought to continue the monopoly in spite of legislative action."[14]

On April 28, 1887, Chicago gas producers organized the Chicago Gas
Trust Company. Formed under Illinois's general incorporation law, the
company's charter allowed it to conduct "the general business of furnishing light, heat and power, from gas . . . in the city of Chicago or elsewhere
in the State of Illinois." The charter also allowed the company "to pur-

chase and hold or sell the capital stock or property of any gas . . . compan[y] in Chicago or elsewhere in Illinois." The Chicago Gas Trust Company operated as a holding company. It held nearly all the stock of the city's four primary gas providers: the Chicago Gas Light and Coke Company; the Peoples Gas Light and Coke Company; the Consumers Gas Company; and the Equitable Gas Light and Fuel Company. In turn, three of these companies held majority interests in Chicago's smaller suburban firms. As I mentioned previously, the Chicago Gas Light and Coke Company owned the Suburban Gas Company. The Consumers Gas Company owned the Lake Gas Company and the Hyde Park Gas Company. Peoples Gas operated the Illinois Light, Heat and Power Company. The Calumet Gas Company, a small Hyde Park concern, was the only operation the Chicago Gas Trust Company did not control.[15]

The holding company served two ends. First, it allowed Chicago gas companies to exploit scale economies. Second, it allowed gas companies to suppress the price competition that followed the introduction of water gas.

Investors believed that the holding company would increase firm profitability. With the formation of the holding company, the market value of Chicago gas companies rose. Between January and March 1887, the stock price of the Chicago Gas Light and Coke Company rose by 50 percent, from 108 to 160. Between October and December 1886, the stock price of the Peoples Gas Light and Coke Company rose by over 200 percent, from 8 to 29. Unlike its anticipated effect on firm profitability, the holding company had an ambiguous effect on consumer welfare. On Chicago's north and south sides, the Chicago Gas Trust Company increased its rate from $1.00 to $1.25. On the city's west side, the company reduced its rate from $1.50 to $1.25.[16]

Market Entry, 1888–97

Market entry continued throughout the late 1880s and early 1890s. However, Chicago gas producers again tried to suppress price competition by combining with the new entrants. In 1889, the Mutual Fuel Gas Company organized. The Mutual's franchise prohibited it from operating outside Hyde Park. After 1889, the Mutual Company tried to amend its original franchise so that it could lay mains outside Hyde Park. When this failed, the owners of the Mutual Company incorporated the Universal Gas Company. On July 23, 1894, the city council granted the Universal Gas Company a fifty-year franchise that included the right to operate anywhere in the city. According to the *Chicago Tribune* (July 18, 1894, 2), the stock price of the gas trust fell two and quarter points "on the passage of the ordinance." When it began operations, the Universal Gas Company owned the largest gas manufacturing plant in the world.

Despite its formidable first impression, the Universal Gas Company never became a competitor of the Chicago Gas Trust. By the fall of 1894, the Universal Company and the gas trust had agreed to divide the city into separate market shares. Through the arrangement, Universal Gas sold nearly all its output to the gas trust and had a "limited number" of private customers. According to the *Tribune,* Wall Street construed the agreement as a victory for the trust. The trust's stock price rose by over six points.[17]

In 1890, the Chicago Economic Fuel Gas Company organized. The company planned to run a natural gas pipeline from Indiana to the Chicago area. Natural gas was typically used as a heating and cooking fuel. In December 1890, the city council granted the company a twenty-five-year franchise, which allowed the company to sell only fuel gas. In July 1891, the city council amended the franchise so that the company could also sell illuminating gas. This created the possibility that the company would compete with the gas trust. Even after the amendment, however, the Economic Company rented all its mains from the gas trust. Early in 1892, the owners of the gas trust gained control over the Economic Company by purchasing most of its outstanding stock.[18]

In March 1895, the Chicago City Council granted a franchise to the Ogden Gas Company. The fifty-year franchise allowed the company to install mains throughout the city. The Ogden Company was the last and perhaps most infamous gas company to enter Chicago. As the story goes, the city council granted the Ogden Company a franchise so the company's founders, which included several prominent Chicago politicians, could sell the franchise to the gas trust. The franchise was extortionate. If the gas trust did not purchase the franchise from its owners, the Ogden would enter the trust's territory. The backers of the Ogden included several members of the city council; Roger Sullivan, a Democratic boss and eventually the company's president; John P. Hopkins, Chicago's mayor; and John W. Lanehart, a cousin of Illinois governor John P. Altgeld. When Lanehart died in 1896, Altgeld acquired his cousin's financial interest in the company.[19]

During the 1890s, three other companies contemplated entering. However, they never carried out their plans. In the summer of 1893, the Continental Gas Company of Chicago was incorporated. One year later, producers planned to organize the Plant Gas Company. In the fall of 1894, the Citizens Co-operative Gas Company was incorporated. The company intended that its stock would be "distributed in small amounts among consumers, instead of being owned by a few capitalists."[20]

Comparisons

The general pattern observed in Chicago—the introduction of water gas, followed by entry and intense price competition, followed by consolidation—mirrored the experience of other cities. Consider Atlanta. The Atlanta Gas Light Company began operations during the 1850s. It dominated the city's gas market until the organization of the Gate City Gas Light Company in 1883. Unlike its older competitor, which sold ordinary coal gas, the Gate City Company sold water gas. Within a year, gas prices in Atlanta fell by 25 percent. By 1889, however, a group of investors from Philadelphia had purchased both companies, consolidated their operations and stabilized prices.[21]

New York, like Chicago, supported multiple gas companies before the introduction of water gas. By 1870, five gas companies operated in the city. They suppressed competition by serving separate districts in the city or by holding financial interests in each another. During the late 1870s, however, two of these companies switched from older methods of production to the manufacture of water gas. With their new and superior technology, they launched an aggressive campaign to capture market share. They began laying mains in their competitors' territories. In some areas of the city, prices fell by 40 percent in a single year. By 1880, gas producers in New York had created a pool, agreeing not to charge less than $2.25 per MCF and not to lay mains in each other's territory. The organization in 1882 of the Equitable Gas Light Company, another water gas producer, threatened to disrupt the pooling arrangement. Equitable began laying a competitive main system. In response, members of the pool tried to devise a more secure form of combination. The creation of the Consolidated Gas Company of New York followed. The Consolidated Company eventually gained control over the city's entire gas market. Similar stories can be told for Baltimore, Buffalo, Cleveland, and many other cities.[22]

Summary

As I noted earlier, the natural monopoly interpretation of utility regulation maintains that competition has not historically worked very well. Attempts to promote competition typically led to brief periods of market entry and price cutting surrounded by longer, sustained periods of monopoly power. The Chicago school paints a more optimistic picture. As an indication of the viability of competition, Jarrell (1978, 273) points to the "profligate franchise-granting activities" of municipal authorities like the Chicago City Council. Jarrell observes that between 1882 and 1905, Chicago granted more than forty franchises to new electric companies.

In the Chicago gas industry, competition had mixed results. Although market entry and the threat of entry kept prices and firm profitability lower than they otherwise would have been, producers still had substantial market power. Combining with their new competitors, gas companies often managed to forestall effective competition. Some observers claimed, with good cause, that members of the city council granted competitive franchises merely to extort bribes from incumbent firms.

Chicago's experiment with competing gas companies began with a technological change. The introduction of water gas lowered the costs of entry and attracted several new gas companies to the city. Market entry and a new, more efficient technology combined to reduce gas prices. This set in motion a wave of institutional changes. The first of these changes was the formation of a holding company. By organizing the holding company, producers hoped to forestall competition and further reductions in gas rates. However, by increasing gas rates, the holding company would engender further changes. The next chapter explores these changes.

CHAPTER 4

Antitrust, 1888–97

The Chicago Citizen's Association was the city's first municipal reform organization. Prominent Chicagoans organized the association in 1874 after two fires destroyed the downtown business district. Working through the association, they hoped to improve the city's firefighting abilities. By the late 1880s, a host of issues interested the association. High on its list was the gas trust's 25 percent rate increase on the city's north and south sides.[1]

On February 4, 1888, the president of the Chicago Citizen's Association, Francis B. Peabody, met with the Illinois attorney general, George Hunt. Peabody tried to convince Hunt to file suit and break up the gas trust. The attorney general sympathized but said that he could do nothing without financial assistance. A few days later, the citizen's association pledged its financial support. Eventually, the association hired James Edsall, a former state's attorney general, to serve as Hunt's special counsel.[2]

With the support of the citizen's association, the attorney general filed a quo warranto suit against the gas trust. Through quo warranto proceedings, states could dissolve corporations that violated their corporate charters or performed other illegal acts. The Chicago Gas Trust was not the only trust subjected to a quo warranto prosecution during the late 1880s and early 1890s. Other states sued Standard Oil, the sugar trust, and the whiskey trust.[3]

A complex and protracted legal battle followed. On May 21, 1889, Judge Baker of the Chicago circuit court maintained the legality of the holding company. The *Tribune*'s financial page reported that the decision caused "a little boom" in the company's stock. Following the decision, the company's stock rose by two and a half percent, on heavy trading.[4] (Using an event study, appendix B explores the financial effects of this and other court decisions.)

On November 26, 1889, the Illinois Supreme Court reversed Judge Baker's ruling and ordered the dissolution of the Chicago Gas Trust Company. Writing for the high court, Justice Magruder ruled that "So far as the appellee was organized with the object of purchasing . . . all the shares of . . . stock of any gas company in Chicago . . . it was not organized for a lawful purpose, and all acts done by it toward the accomplishment of such object are illegal and void." Magruder explained that the holding company granted Chicago gas producers "a virtual monopoly in the manufacture and sale of gas" and whatever creates "a monopoly is unlawful" and "contrary to public policy." The decision shocked investors. Between November 26 and 30, the holding company's stock fell by nearly 25 percent.[5]

In March 1890, the Chicago Gas Trust Company requested that the Illinois Supreme Court rehear the case. The court denied the request. Also, a Chicago lawyer, F. M. Charlton, brought proceedings against the gas trust. Charlton petitioned the courts "to appoint a receiver to take charge of and sell the property" of the trust. He also asked for an injunction restraining the combination from selling any of its assets or paying any dividends. On May 28, 1890, the court announced that it would appoint a receiver for the trust. A month later, however, Charlton dropped his suit.[6] Charlton's motivations remain a mystery.

In the late summer of 1890, Illinois brought another suit against the holding company. The state filed this second suit because the supreme court's first decision held that it was illegal for the Chicago Gas Trust Company to hold "*all* the shares of . . . stock of any gas company in Chicago [emphasis added]." The court did not rule that it was illegal to hold smaller interests. This second suit challenged the gas trust's ability to hold even a single share of another company's stock. In September, a Chicago circuit court ruled against a motion by the Chicago Gas Company to have the state's (second) suit dismissed. In November, a trial court "entered a sweeping order forever disbarring the [Chicago Gas Trust Company] from holding any stock, even a minority, in any other gas company." While all of this litigation had been taking place, the Chicago Gas Trust Company continued to operate as a holding company. However, the company dropped the word *trust* from its name in April 1890.[7]

Getting around the Law

Because of the state's second quo warranto action, the Chicago Gas Company announced that it would restructure itself. Producers considered three reorganization plans. First, they considered reorganizing under a New Jersey charter. The next section will consider why producers rejected the New Jersey plan. Second, producers discussed merging the holding company's constituent firms into a single Illinois corporation under the title of the Peoples Gas Light and Coke Company. Producers also rejected this plan. Third, the management of the holding company considered, and eventually adopted, a plan to reorganize as a bona fide trust. According to the *Tribune,* this plan faced the fewest legal obstacles.[8]

A trust's teleology resembled a holding company's. The holding company was a corporation chartered to hold stock in other corporations. Because the holding company had a financial interest in all its member firms, it subordinated the economic interests of the individual firms to their combined profitability. The holding company helped the constituent firms collude. A trust accomplished the identical end. Hovenkamp (1991, 250) describes a trust:

> In a stock-transfer trust the holders of stock in different corporations entered into common law trust agreements transferring their shares to a common group of trustees in exchange for "trust certificates," reflecting the ownership interest of each individual shareholder. The trustees were obligated by the trust agreement to vote the shares according to the wishes of the trust certificate owners. The trustees then made management decisions for all the participating corporations together, and the boards of directors of each corporation were obligated to vote according to the trustees' orders.

The state's antitrust suits had only a negligible effect on the Chicago gas industry. The similarity between a holding company and a trust helps explain why. (Appendix B analyzes how the state's antitrust suits affected prices and market structure.)

On April 9, 1891, the Chicago Gas Company surrendered its corporate charter and restructured itself as a trust.[9] The newly organized trust held the stock of all the companies that had previously made up the holding company: the Chicago Gas Light and Coke Company, the Peoples Gas Light and Coke Company, the Consumers Gas Company and the Equitable Gas Light and Fuel Company. These companies controlled all the smaller suburban concerns in the Chicago area, except the Calumet Gas Company and the Mutual Fuel Gas Company.

Chicago gas producers also continued to combine through interlocking directorship and management schemes. In June 1891, C. E. Judson was president of the Consumers Gas Company, the Hyde Park Gas Company, and the Lake Gas Company. C. F. Bryant was the secretary of all three companies. C. K. G. Billings was the vice president of the Chicago Gas Light and Coke Company and president of both the Peoples Gas Light and Coke Company and the Suburban Gas Company. G. A. Yullie was the secretary of the Chicago Gas Light and Coke Company, the Suburban Gas Company, and the Equitable Gas Light and Fuel Company.[10]

Why Producers Did Not Reorganize in New Jersey

Between 1888 and 1896, New Jersey passed a series of liberal incorporation laws. By 1893, New Jersey law allowed a business to make the state its
legal domicile without physically moving its assets there. New Jersey
hoped that by creating a legal environment friendly to corporations it
would attract new businesses to the state and increase its tax revenues. The
strategy worked. The number of firms incorporating themselves in New
Jersey grew rapidly, as did the state's tax revenue. By 1904, more than half
the state's tax revenue came from incorporation fees and franchise taxes.
New Jersey's liberal incorporation laws proved especially attractive to
industrial combinations prosecuted under state antitrust laws. The gas
trust aside, every combination and trust dissolved by state quo warranto
suits during the 1890s reorganized as a New Jersey corporation.[11]

What stopped the Chicago Gas Trust Company from pursuing the
popular New Jersey plan? According to the *Chicago Tribune* (November
30, 1889, 1), even if the Chicago holding company resurrected itself as a
New Jersey corporation, the charters of its constituent companies, which
were all Illinois corporations, would have remained subject to state
antitrust prosecution.

Another possible explanation centers on New Jersey's gas act. Passed
in 1874 and amended in 1876, New Jersey's gas act was an incorporation
law for gas companies. Gas companies had to incorporate under the gas
act. They could not incorporate under the state's general incorporation
law. Moreover, unlike the general incorporation law, the gas act imposed
stringent requirements on individuals who wanted to incorporate gas companies. For example, the act required that the backers of a potential company have raised one half of its proposed capital stock before incorporating the company.[12]

Incumbent gas companies sometimes used the gas act to prevent market entry. For example, the Jersey City Gas Company sued to prevent the
Consumers Gas Company of Jersey City from organizing. Jersey City Gas
claimed that the Consumers Company failed to meet the obligations of the
gas act; the proposed company apparently had not yet raised enough capital. The court agreed, and the Jersey City Gas Company retained its
monopoly position. Similarly, in *Richards v. Dover,* the Dover Gaslight,
Heat & Power Company asked the court to set aside a municipal franchise.
The franchise granted the Dover Electric Company the exclusive privilege
of manufacturing and distributing gas in Dover. Dover Electric was incorporated under the general incorporation act, not the gas act. Dover
Gaslight claimed that the city could not grant a franchise to distribute gas

to a company organized under the general incorporation act. New Jersey's supreme court agreed and set aside the ordinance.[13]

If Chicago gas companies wanted to reorganize under New Jersey law, they would have had to incorporate themselves under the gas act, not the state's liberal incorporation law. The case of *Seattle Gas v. Citizens' Light & Power Co.* illustrates this fact. The Seattle Gas Company was incorporated under the laws of the state of Washington. It asked for an injunction preventing the Citizens' Company from operating in the city of Seattle. The case hinged on the fact that the Citizens' Company incorporated under New Jersey's general incorporation law, not the gas act. The Citizens' Company argued that because it operated outside the state of New Jersey it was not obligated to organize under the gas act. A federal court disagreed and granted the Seattle Gas Company its injunction. The court blocked the Citizens' Company from operating in Seattle because it had no authority to manufacture and sell gas in New Jersey, or anywhere else.[14]

The court decided *Seattle* in 1903. As a result, Chicago gas companies may not have fully grasped the legal and organizational implications of the gas act in 1890. This said, Chicago gas companies probably did appreciate some of the risks the act posed.

The State's Response to the Newly Organized Gas Trust

The Chicago Gas Company's legal troubles continued even after it reorganized itself as a bona fide trust. After the gas trust purchased the Chicago Economic Fuel Gas Company in 1892, many Chicago consumers demanded that the city council take action (see chap. 3 for a discussion of the gas trust's acquisition of the Chicago Economic Fuel Gas Company). The *Tribune,* for example, reported that "four hundred indignant citizens" protested the acquisition. In response, on February 29, 1892, the Chicago City Council revoked the franchise of the Chicago Economic Company for violating the conditions of its franchise. The franchise prohibited the Chicago Economic from selling, leasing, or transferring its franchise privileges to any other gas company. Later that year, the courts held that the city council did not possess the authority to revoke the franchise.[15]

In the spring of 1894 the Illinois attorney general prepared another quo warranto suit against the gas trust. The suit culminated in a court of equity decree. The decree restrained the Chicago Gas Light and Coke Company (a company in the trust) from holding any interest in the Suburban Gas Company. The decree also enjoined the companies from issuing any stock to other corporations. Lastly, the decree ordered the dissolution of all unlawful combinations between the several companies in the trust but held that the trust itself was lawful. The *American Gas Light Journal* reported that the decision amounted to "a practical victory for the trust." Consistent with this, the *Tribune* reported that the trust's stock rose when the court announced its decision. In a related action, the Illinois attorney general secured an injunction preventing Chicago gas companies from paying any dividends. The decision forced the trust to reduce its dividend rate in 1895 and 1896, but affected little else.[16]

Responding to this litigation, the owners of the gas trust began searching for an organizational arrangement that would be immune to legal attack. In an interview with the *Tribune,* the attorney for the gas trust explained. Many investors argued that continued legal battles "unsettled" the value of their stock. The trust's attorney went on to argue that the "present organization probably will not hold." As a result, the owners were "determined to wipe out the present organization and create another." On October 1, 1895, the Chicago Gas Company announced that the seven companies in the trust would merge into a single firm. Initially, market observers expressed optimism over the plan. The *American Gas Light Journal* reported: "A plan for the legal rehabilitation of the Chicago Trust interests has been formulated, and the belief is that it will stand the test of law." Similarly, the *Tribune* reported that the trust's stock rose several points when the market learned of the reorganization plan.[17]

In the spring of 1896, the Chicago Gas Company submitted an application to reorganize. On advice from the attorney general, the secretary of state refused the application. The gas trust initiated mandamus proceedings to compel acceptance. The courts deferred hearing the case until October 1897. As the next chapter will make clear, by October 1897 the issue would be moot (Illinois Bureau of Labor Statistics 1897, 303–4).

Comparisons

Few cities used antitrust enforcement as vigorously as Chicago. The closest parallel appears in Detroit. Formed in 1851, the Detroit Gas Light Company enjoyed a monopoly over Detroit's gas industry until the organization of the Mutual Gas Light Company. Shortly after the Mutual entered the city in 1872, a price war broke-out. Gas rates fell from $3.50 to 50 cents per MCF. Rates rose to $2.25 after the Mutual Company and the Detroit Gas Light Company agreed to divide the city into separate and exclusive market shares. Detroit authorities responded, revoking the Mutual Company's franchise and seizing the company's gas mains and plant. The city maintained that the restrictive agreement violated the Mutual Company's franchise; the franchise prohibited the company from combining with its competitors. The Michigan Supreme Court agreed that the covenant violated the franchise but ruled that the city had to find some remedy other than seizing the company's property.[18]

In 1892, the Detroit Gas Company, a new company, formally absorbed both the Mutual Gas Light Company and the Detroit Gas Light Company. The consolidation of these companies gave the Detroit Gas Company a monopoly. Detroit's mayor, Hazen Pingree, launched a four-pronged response. First, Pingree lobbied the state legislature for a law empowering the city to regulate gas rates. The gas company did some lobbying of its own and defeated the law. Second, Pingree threatened to allow a new company to enter the city if Detroit Gas did not reduce its rate. He was bluffing and the company knew it. Gas rates stayed the same. Third, Pingree sued the Mutual Gas Light Company for damages because the company had for five years charged consumers a rate over that dictated by its franchise. The court ruled in favor of Pingree. The gas company had to refund its excess charges. Fourth, Pingree discovered that a key franchise held by the Detroit Gas Company had expired several years earlier. Without this franchise, the company had no authority to operate in the city. Pingree had the company dead to rights, and the company knew it. Detroit Gas stock plummeted, from 80 cents a share to 15 cents a share. Threatened with legal extinction, the Detroit Gas Company agreed to reduce its rates from $1.25 to $1.00.[19]

Antitrust aside, the regulatory dynamics observed in Chicago were representative. Consider the example that ended the last chapter, the formation of the Consolidated Gas Company of New York. Recall that the Consolidated Company merged several competing firms. Shortly after its formation, the Consolidated cut its rates from $2.25 to $1.75. Simultaneously, however, it reduced the quality of its gas. Some customers claimed that the reduction in quality induced them to use so much more gas that their bills went up, despite the reduction in rates. Although the accuracy of these claims remains unclear, merchants, small businesses, and other customers organized a group called the Gas Consumers' Association of New York. The association, and other large individual gas consumers, pushed the state legislature to reduce the rates charged by the Consolidated. After a lengthy investigation, the legislature passed a law requiring that rates be reduced from $1.75 to $1.25. The association also lobbied the state's attorney general to file suit dissolving the company. Little came of this, however. A small survey of other cities reveals similar patterns in Baltimore, Peoria (Illinois), and St. Louis.[20]

Summary

Three aspects of Chicago's experience with antitrust regulation speak to the larger argument here. First, as North's (1990) theory suggests, relative price changes animated institutional change. For example, after the gas trust increased rates on the city's north and south sides, consumers initiated an antitrust suit against the trust. Second, unlike other industrial trusts during the late nineteenth century, the Chicago gas trust could not escape state antitrust prosecution by reorganizing itself in New Jersey. Rather than having a onetime court battle with the state's attorney and moving on, the gas trust had to stay and fight it out in the courts. Third, consumer agitation, not the lobbying efforts of smaller manufacturers, drove antitrust regulation in Chicago.[21]

CHAPTER 5

Monopoly, 1897–1905

Market entry and litigation drove Chicago gas companies to lobby for the gas acts. Passed in 1897, the gas acts consisted of two laws: the Lowenthal Street Frontage Act and the Gas Consolidation Act. The consolidation act removed the court-erected obstacles to merger and combination. Under the frontage act, before laying any mains, gas companies had to secure permission from the property owners who held land fronting the street or alley where they wanted to install mains. The frontage act created a prohibitive entry barrier. By bribing property owners to oppose new main construction, incumbent gas companies could prevent entry.

Senator Miller of Cook County first introduced the street frontage bill in 1895. The 1895 version of the frontage bill prohibited local governments from granting a franchise "for the laying of gas pipes . . . without the consent of the owners of more than one-half of the property fronting the street or alley along which it is . . . proposed to lay the pipes." Although the house and senate both passed the bill, Governor Altgeld vetoed the measure. Altgeld maintained that "In no instance has the public asked for the passage of this bill. The Chicago gas companies labored for its passage."[1]

In 1897, Illinois lawmakers introduced a new version of the street frontage bill and another measure, the gas consolidation bill. Besides the provisions set forth in the 1895 frontage bill, the 1897 bill "made it possible for a person with the smallest interest in a piece of property facing a street or alley to go into court and block the laying of pipes." This provision strengthened the frontage bill. Instead of having to convince several owners of abutting property to oppose main construction, now an incumbent gas company needed to sway only one property owner or purchase a small piece of land itself to block entry. The consolidation bill contained twelve sections. The first two sections are most relevant. The first section authorized any Illinois gas company "to sell, transfer, convey or lease" its property, charters, and franchises to any other gas company. The second section stated that "It shall be lawful for any gas companies now organized or hereafter to be organized in this State, doing business in the same city, town or village, to consolidate and merge into a single corporation, which shall be one of said merging and consolidating corporations, by complying with the provisions of this act hereinafter specified." The other sections specified the prerequisites of consolidation. The bill, for example, prohibited companies from increasing prices during the year following a merger.[2]

Chicago gas companies worked hard for the gas acts. One state senator maintained that the attorney for the gas trust wrote the consolidation bill. Several Chicago papers suggested that gas companies used bribery to garner support. As one reporter colorfully phrased it, "the price of legislators was as freely discussed . . . as the price of hogs at the stockyards." Other observers estimated that lobbyists could purchase a legislator's support with $1,500.[3]

Municipal reform groups opposed the gas acts. For example, in one publication, the Civic Federation of Chicago maintained that "these two gas bills are to be taken as one, as they are closely allied and are being pushed by the same forces and for the same purpose, viz.: to give the Gas Trust everything it wants and to give the public nothing in return." The federation also organized a public rally to protest the gas acts.[4]

On May 19, 1897, the senate defeated the consolidation and frontage bills. Gas producers lobbied to have the bills reconsidered. The *Tribune* reported: "The friends of the gas bills are working tonight to line up their forces and put the measures through. They will probably succeed in this." The paper was right. The legislature reconsidered the bills and on June 1, 1897, the legislature passed the Gas Consolidation Act and the Street Frontage Act. The senate passed the frontage act by a vote of thirty-one to thirteen. It passed the consolidation act by a vote of twenty-nine to seventeen. The house passed the frontage act by a vote of ninety to forty-nine. It passed the consolidation act by a vote of eighty-nine to fifty-two. Governor Tanner signed the bills into law a short time later.[5]

Why were the gas acts defeated on the first vote and then passed by sizable majorities a short time later? The *Tribune* (May 20, 1897, 2) offered one plausible explanation:

> There are some funny things in connection with these bills, judging by the actions of some people in and around the General Assembly. Intimations are heard that there is a big stock-jobbing scheme in it, and that the bills are being manipulated to break the market.

By the *Tribune*'s reasoning, insiders would have bought the gas trust's stock right after the first vote defeating the gas bills. Presumably, following the defeat of the bills, the price of the trust's stock would have been very low. A few days later, after the legislature passed the bills, stock prices would have been higher. The insiders then would have sold their recently purchased stock and made a killing.

The number of trades and the behavior of stock prices on May 19, the day the gas bills failed to pass, are consistent with the *Tribune*'s "stock-jobbing" explanation. The *Tribune*'s financial page explained (May 20, 1897, 9):

> of a total of 150,000 shares dealt in on the [stock] exchange for the day . . . Chicago Gas alone . . . [was] credited with 63,000 shares. A large proportion of these sales was made in the last hour and a half of the trading, and enormous blocks of stock were unloaded with precipitate eagerness which had been bought in the conviction that the consolidation bill would succeed. The price, which had advanced a point in the morning, tumbled along 3 and a half percent.

The Consolidation of the Chicago Gas Industry

After the gas acts, producers began consolidating their control over the gas industry. In August of 1897, all of the companies that had previously been members of the gas trust merged under the title of the Peoples Gas Light and Coke Company. During the next two years, the Peoples Gas Company acquired the Calumet Gas Company, the Mutual Fuel Gas Company, and the Hyde Park Gas Company. Acquiring the Mutual Company and Hyde Park Company gave Peoples Gas a monopoly over gas production in Hyde Park. With its new-found market power, Peoples Gas increased rates in Hyde Park from 72 cents to $1 per MCF. Several Hyde Park residents sought an injunction preventing the increase. An Illinois appellate court denied the injunction.[6]

The franchises of the Universal Gas Company and the Ogden Gas Company prohibited them from combining with any other gas company. Consequently, the Peoples Gas Light and Coke Company could not formally purchase these companies until the city council amended their franchises, allowing them to combine with other gas companies. Without these amendments, Peoples Gas had to control the Universal and Ogden gas companies through informal collusive arrangements.

In December 1897, Peoples Gas and Ogden Gas agreed to divide Chicago into two separate and exclusive market shares. Under the agreement, Peoples Gas reportedly paid the Ogden Company $60,000 a year to restrict its operations to a small area on the city's north side. In return for this payment and the promise that it would not invade Ogden's north side territory, the Peoples Gas Company enjoyed exclusive control over the rest of the city's gas market (*Chicago Tribune,* September 12, 1900, 7).

In April 1900, Peoples Gas approached the owners of Ogden Gas with an offer to purchase the company. The owners of the Peoples Company planned to purchase Ogden Gas themselves, acting as individual investors, not collectively as a corporation. In this way, the Peoples Gas Light and Coke Company would not own Ogden Gas. Rather, the owners of the Peoples Company would own it. While the distinction seems trivial, it would have allowed Peoples Gas to get around the provisions in Ogden's franchise prohibiting it from directly combining with any other gas company.

Apparently, Ogden's owners set their asking price too high. Peoples Gas decided not buy. Instead, the Peoples Company devised a predatory pricing scheme to lower Ogden's asking price. The company organized a front company known as the Municipal Gas Company. The Municipal Company leased all its mains and purchased all its gas from the Peoples Gas Light and Coke Company. Municipal was a sort of fighting brand, analogous to those used by American Tobacco and Standard Oil in their predatory pricing schemes. Peoples Gas used the Municipal Company to price below cost *only* in the territory of Ogden Gas. Prices in other areas of the city were not lowered. The scheme drove the Ogden Company into a precarious financial position and allowed Peoples Gas to acquire its assets at distress values.[7]

In August 1900, the Municipal Gas Company initiated a price war with the Ogden Gas Company. Gas prices fell by 60 percent within a month. First the Municipal Gas Company cut its price from $1 to 60 cents per MCF. Then the Ogden Company reduced its price from 90 cents to 60 cents. Prices eventually fell to 40 cents. The price war was concentrated in an area of roughly fifteen square miles. As the *Tribune* described it, "The disputed territory in which the gas war is raging extends from Division street to Fullerton avenue and from the lake to the Northwestern tracks" (see the map in fig. 2). As gas prices fell, so too did the stock price of the Ogden Gas Company. With the decline in stock prices, investors saw a bargain and approached the Ogden Company with offers to buy. By October 20, 1900, the president of the Mutual Gas Company, Alexander Hamilton, and the owners of the Ogden Company had settled on the terms of a sale. Within days, the price war ceased and Municipal Gas shut down, never to be heard from again.[8]

On November 1, 1900, Hamilton and a syndicate of buyers friendly to the Peoples Gas Company purchased a 75 percent share in the Ogden Gas Company. Roger Sullivan, a powerful Democratic boss, retained a 25 percent share in the Ogden Company. As part of the deal, the Peoples Company guaranteed $6 million of Ogden's bonds. Peoples Gas also contracted to purchase the plant, mains, and all other property of Ogden Gas in 1945, when Ogden's franchise expired. Under the contract, in 1945, Peoples Gas would pay $7 million for Ogden's property. When the deal between Ogden Gas and the Peoples Gas syndicate was made public in early 1901, Chicago authorities threatened to sieze the Ogden's plant and mains for violating its franchise. Nothing ever came of these threats, however. The Ogden continued to operate as a de facto subsidiary of the Peoples Gas Company. City authorities made similar noises when they learned of the informal ties between the Universal Gas Company and Peoples Gas Company. Again, however, there was much ado about nothing. (Chapter 2 describes the collusive arrangement between the Universal Gas Company and the Chicago Gas Company, the predecessor of Peoples Gas.)[9]

In 1906, the Chicago City Council enacted an ordinance allowing the Peoples Gas Company to formally purchase the Ogden and Universal companies. (The next chapter describes this ordinance in more detail.) In 1907, with the last remaining barriers to merger and consolidation removed, Peoples Gas leased "all the plants, properties, and business" of the Universal and Ogden gas companies. The leases extended to 1944 and 1945 when the franchises of the Universal and Ogden companies expired, respectively. In 1914, the Peoples Gas Company commuted the present value of all future rental and cash payments into one lump sum. With this, Peoples Gas effectively purchased both companies, acquiring full "right, title and interest" to their property.[10]

Clarence Darrow, Roger Sullivan, and Consumer Agitation

The price war between the Ogden Gas Company and the Municipal Gas Company outraged consumers who lived outside the Ogden's north side territory. How was it that Peoples Gas, acting through the Municipal Company, charged north side consumers only 40 cents per MCF, while consumers elsewhere had to pay $1? What justified such discrimination? In the city's thirtieth ward, three hundred "property owners and householders" met "to protest against the alleged discrimination of the Peoples Gas company." In the thirty-third ward, consumers formed the Anti-Gas Trust Association to equalize gas rates across the city. On the city's south side, five hundred consumers organized the South Side Gas Consumers' Protective Association. The association urged the city council to reduce gas rates.[11]

Roger Sullivan of the Ogden Gas Company subsidized one act of consumer protest. Soon after Peoples Gas invaded Ogden's territory, Sullivan pulled together several prominent Chicagoans, among them famed attorney Clarence Darrow. Sullivan requested that they speak out against the Peoples Gas Company and the gas acts. So that his friends would have a place to be heard, Sullivan rented the Central Music Hall, a large auditorium, for the evening of September 27, 1900. He also purchased a large stash of fireworks. When the 27th arrived, Sullivan set off the fireworks on the streets surrounding the music hall to attract as many people as he could.[12]

At the music hall, Clarence Darrow railed against the gas acts. He argued that the consolidation act "had been secured by bribery." He pleaded for the repeal of the frontage act, "which he explained prevented the establishment of any more gas companies in Chicago." According to Darrow, if other areas of the city had experienced competing gas companies, they also would have enjoyed low gas rates. During the meeting, another of Sullivan's speakers announced the formation of a committee, which included Darrow and other prominent Chicago attorneys, to bring suit against Peoples Gas.[13]

Darrow drafted a petition against the Peoples Gas Light and Coke Company. The petition asked that the courts require the company to charge all its customers, not just those on the north side, 40 cents per MCF. Although the petition failed, Darrow succeeded in pushing the state's attorney general to initiate a quo warranto suit against Peoples Gas. The state's suit challenged the constitutionality of the Gas Consolidation Act on two grounds: first, that the law was improperly titled, and second, that the law granted the Peoples Gas Light and Coke Company privileges not available to other corporations in the state. Peoples Gas derived its legitimacy from the consolidation act. If the courts declared the act unconstitutional, the company would have been vulnerable to dissolution. The Illinois Supreme Court, however, ruled that the consolidation act was constitutional.[14]

Historians typically paint very different pictures of Clarence Darrow and Roger Sullivan. Darrow was the dedicated lawyer who fought for social justice and reform. Sullivan was the powerful and corrupt political boss. What could have motivated Darrow to speak and act in favor of a cause so dear to Sullivan? It was probably a marriage of convenience. Darrow and Sullivan both wanted the same thing: to punish the Peoples Gas Light and Coke Company for charging discriminatory rates. A sense of justice animated Darrow. A different sense animated Sullivan.[15]

How Local Politicians Responded to Agitation and the Gas Acts

The city council considered a series of measures to placate gas consumers. The Chicago City Council convened for the first time after its summer recess on September 24, 1900. At that meeting, the council introduced nine ordinances. All nine dealt with the gas question. Some ordinances requested the Illinois legislature and/or attorney general repeal the gas acts. Other ordinances asked the state legislature to grant the city permission to build a municipal gas plant. Still another fixed the maximum price of gas in Chicago at 75 cents per MCF.[16]

The 75-cent rate ordinance faced three obstacles. First, Mayor Carter Harrison opposed the measure. Harrison argued that "any ordinance giving the Council the power to determine the price of gas will, sooner or later, become a sandbag in the hands of dishonest and blackmailing aldermen." Second, even the city's own attorneys were not sure that the city council actually had the authority to regulate gas rates. Finally, in selecting a 75-cent rate, the city made no inquiry into the actual costs of producing and distributing coal gas. Such arbitrariness would make court enforcement that much more difficult once producers challenged the ordinance.[17]

Despite these problems, on October 15, 1900, the city council passed the 75-cent ordinance. The vote was unanimous. The Peoples Gas Light and Coke Company refused to comply with the ordinance. The company sued in a federal court. The company claimed that the 75-cent rate should be enjoined because the city did not have the authority to regulate gas rates. On appeal, the U.S. Supreme Court denied the company any relief because the federal courts did not have jurisdiction. A stockholder of the gas company, Darius O. Mills, also sued in federal court. Like the company, he challenged the city's authority to regulate rates. Because Mills resided in another state, namely California, the federal courts could claim jurisdiction.[18]

In *Mills v. City of Chicago*, a federal court granted the injunction. The court ruled: "the regulation of the prices to charge consumers by gas companies is not one of the powers essential to municipal government, and is not included in general powers conferred on cities." The court explained that unless the state constitution, or the legislature, explicitly granted regulatory powers to city governments, such powers could only be exercised by the state: "and such power cannot be exercised by a city unless it has been delegated by the state in express words, or by fair implication from a power expressly granted." Chicago authorities appealed to the U.S. Supreme Court. They claimed that Mills and Peoples Gas colluded in bringing the suit. Apparently, another large stockholder of the Peoples Gas Company admitted giving Mills $5,000 to help defray his legal expenses. The Supreme Court upheld the lower court's ruling. The city council lacked the authority to regulate gas rates until the state legislature expressly delegated that authority.[19]

A Digression: Justice Magruder, Judicial Politics, and the Gas Trust

In 1903, when the Illinois Supreme Court ruled that the Gas Consolidation Act was constitutional, a single justice—Justice Magruder—dissented. In

1887, Magruder refused to enforce the restrictive covenant between the Chicago Gas Light and Coke Company and the Peoples Gas Light and Coke Company. In 1889, Magruder wrote a scathing opinion against the gas trust in *People v. Chicago Gas Trust.* What forces shaped Magruder's consistent opposition to Chicago gas companies?

The state appointed Benjamin D. Magruder to the Illinois Supreme Court in 1885 after the unexpected death of Justice Lyle Dickey. Magruder was then elected to the high court in 1888 and reelected in 1897. He served as the court's chief justice for much of the 1890s. His tenure as an Illinois Supreme Court justice ended in 1906, when he lost his bid for reelection. While he held office, Magruder represented Illinois's seventh supreme court district. As noted in chapter 2, the Illinois Supreme Court consisted of seven justices, each representing a distinct electoral district. Importantly, the seventh district consisted almost entirely of Chicago voters. In the words of one *Tribune* reporter, Magruder was "Chicago's judge."[20]

Very little has been written about Magruder's career. Not until his electoral defeat in 1906 did he even attract much attention from the Chicago press. In April 1906, Magruder's supporters organized a committee of prominent Chicagoans to push for his reelection. Members of the committee included Clarence Darrow and Francis B. Peabody. Darrow tried to get the consolidation act declared unconstitutional. Peabody helped sponsor Illinois's quo warranto suit against the gas trust. The committee to reelect Magruder organized a mass meeting to rally the support of Chicago voters. The committee also flooded the city with pamphlets describing Magruder's many decisions in favor of Chicago citizens. His decisions against the gas trust figured prominently, as did his decisions against the whiskey trust and the sugar trust—while Magruder was a justice, the Illinois Supreme Court ousted the whiskey trust and the sugar trust from the state.[21]

Magruder's campaign divided the local press. The *Chicago American,* a Hearst paper, supported Magruder. The paper argued that "[h]e decided against the trusts and in favor of the people." The paper went on to explain that "the corporations" opposed Magruder's reelection "because of his anti-trust decisions." The *Tribune* seemed to take a neutral stance. The *Chicago Record-Herald* opposed Magruder. In an editorial, the *Record-Herald* expressed two concerns. The first was Magruder's age. He was 68 at a time when the life expectancy of a native-born white male at age 10 was about 50. The second was his antagonistic personality. According to the paper, Magruder had alienated many of his fellow justices.[22]

Magruder's campaign also divided the Democratic Party. One faction, led by Edward Dunne, Chicago's mayor in 1906, wanted Magruder to run as a Democrat. Another faction, led by Carter Harrison, wanted W. Fenimore Cooper to run as the Democratic candidate to the high court. The Harrison faction won. Cooper ran as the Democrat, and Magruder ran as an independent. The schism within the Democratic Party proved fatal for both Magruder and Cooper. In the final election, voters split between Cooper and Magruder. Cooper received 26,387 votes; Magruder received 26,696 votes. The Republican candidate Orrin N. Carter won 48,921 votes. The *Tribune* explained the results: "the contest over the Supreme court judgeship does not seem to have been between the republicans and democrats at all. The returns indicate the fight was between the [Dunne] and Harrison factions of the democrats and while they were squabbling Judge Carter simply walked in." Magruder's electoral loss in 1906 contrasts markedly with his victory in 1897. In 1897, Magruder won 120,581 of the 124,672 votes cast.[23]

The Effects of the Gas Acts

Four pieces of evidence suggest that the gas acts promoted monopoly. First, between 1880 and 1897, a new firm entered the Chicago gas industry once every two years. After 1897, market entry ceased. Second, investors believed that the gas acts would increase firm profitability. An event study reveals that the market value of Chicago gas companies rose with passage of the gas acts. Appendix B describes the event study in detail. Observations from the financial press corroborate the event study results. See, for example, my earlier discussion of the passage of the gas acts and the reaction of the stock market.

Third, before 1897, nominal gas prices in Chicago fell steadily. After 1897, they stopped falling. Certainly factors other than the gas acts may have caused gas prices to stop falling. To control for at least some of these other factors, I compare gas prices in Chicago to gas prices in a sample of other U.S. cities. These other cities were similar to Chicago except that their regulatory environments remained constant; they did not secure passage of laws like the gas acts. These cities act as a control group. Over time, changes in the ratio of Chicago gas prices to prices in these other cities should filter out industrywide price changes and help isolate the effects of the gas acts. The ratio of prices in Chicago to prices in the control group rose after 1897. More precisely, gas prices in cities that did not pass laws like the gas acts kept on falling after 1897 while gas prices in Chicago stopped falling. Appendix B describes the control group cities and the data.

Finally, in February 1906, several investors approached Mayor Dunne with an offer: give them a fifty-year franchise to make and distribute gas in the city and they would sell it for 60 cents. In February 1906, gas rates in Chicago had just been reduced from $1 to 85 cents per MCF. The mayor, while favorably disposed to the plan, was not hopeful. He explained that the frontage law would likely prevent entry. "As things stand now," the mayor said, "it practically would be impossible for an independent company to secure the necessary frontage consents to allow it to do business if the city council should grant a franchise."[24]

Comparisons

As I noted in the last chapter, few cities pursued antitrust enforcement as vigorously as Chicago. Perhaps as a result, laws like the consolidation act are rare. I can find only one other state that passed similar legislation. In 1906, Maryland passed a law that enabled gas and electric companies in Baltimore to merge under the title, Consolidated Gas, Electric Light, and Power Company of Baltimore City (Wilcox 1910, 625).

Outside Chicago, state and local governments frequently passed frontage laws for all types of utilities. Ostensibly, authorities passed such laws to protect property owners from the reckless acts of utility companies. Surveying frontage laws at the turn of the century, Wilcox (1910, 75–76) writes:

> While there is an element of justice in the theory of property owners' consents, . . . on the whole the plan is a bad one. . . . If property owners' consents are required at all, an alternative should be left open to the franchise holder, if he fails to get the necessary number, to appeal to some judicial tribunal, as is done in New York, for permission to occupy the streets with his fixtures. *The consent law of Ohio has been a desperate failure and has tended to intrench [sic] existing companies in defiance of the public will* [emphasis added].

Gas companies enjoyed regulatory entry barriers beyond frontage laws. In New Jersey, gas companies used the aforementioned gas act to prevent entry. Also, in both Cincinnati and Cleveland, coal gas companies bribed local politicians not to grant franchises to natural gas companies. Similar patterns occurred in other utility industries. For example, in 1899, the Bell System lobbied for a Connecticut law that required all new telephone companies to obtain a special charter from the state legislature. Potential Bell competitors later claimed the law was anticompetitive.[25]

Summary

The gas acts undermined one of the few constraints on the behavior of Chicago gas companies: the market mechanism. After 1897, no new firms entered the industry. The state's antitrust prosecutions ceased. Relative to prices in other U.S. cities, gas prices in Chicago rose. The market value of Chicago gas securities also rose. By the early 1900s, the Peoples Gas Light and Coke Company dominated the city's gas industry.

Earlier institutional changes inspired the gas acts. Producers lobbied for them to prevent continued market entry and antitrust prosecution. The gas acts also inspired further institutional change. The increase in gas rates that followed the gas acts led consumers and local politicians to lobby for further institutional changes that would lower rates. Consumers organized to have the gas acts repealed or declared unconstitutional. They failed. The courts maintained the legitimacy of the gas acts, and the legislature refused to revoke the laws. Consumers also lobbied the Chicago City Council. The city council responded, but it had little success. The courts ruled that the city council exceeded its constitutional authority when it regulated gas rates. As the next chapter will explain, local politicians responded to this setback by securing passage of the Enabling Act, a law that granted them the power to regulate rates.

CHAPTER 6

Municipal Regulation, 1905–13

Mills v. Chicago left no doubt: without a special enabling law, the Chicago City Council had no power to regulate gas rates. Thwarted by the courts, Chicago politicians turned to the state legislature. The legislature responded. In the spring of 1905, the Illinois house held hearings to assess the demand for a municipal regulation law.

Gas companies from Bloomington, Chester, Freeport, Peoria, and Princeton testified against municipal regulation. The representatives of a Peoria gas company argued against municipal regulation on two grounds. First, they claimed that it was in their economic interest to provide good, economical service. Second, they argued that it would be impossible for local officials to take the time and expense necessary to justly fix rates. Companies from the other cities claimed that they were not earning any excess profits and characterized the enabling bills as "vicious measures."[1]

Officials of the Peoples Gas Light and Coke Company also testified. Company officials opposed municipal regulation but were willing to accept state regulation if that would forestall municipal control. James Meagher, legal counsel for the Peoples Gas Company, argued: "By city regulation you place it in the hands of the people interested to sit in judgement of their own case. Despite their protestations of fairness they could not restrain from giving themselves the best of it. Therefore we fear city regulation." Meagher continued: "[W]e do not want to be at the mercy of the city. Let there be a commission appointed, a state commission appointed by the governor. . . . Let this commission examine books and investigate accounts, let the commission fix rates." Roger Sullivan, now president of the Ogden Gas Company, echoed Meagher's sentiments: "We feel that we should have something to say about the regulation and that it should not be left in the hands of a city council to go ahead without any attempt to discover what it costs to manufacture and distribute gas. Of course we don't want anything, but if we have to take something we prefer that a commission, city or state, be created."[2]

According to the *Tribune,* gas companies throughout Illinois actively supported a house bill that would have created a state regulatory commission.[3] State regulation, though, would not arrive until 1914. Why did producers find state regulators more sympathetic to their interests than local regulators? The next chapter argues that low gas rates made more political hay for local regulators than for state regulators.

While producers lobbied against municipal regulation, consumers and local politicians lobbied for it. Evanston, Galesburg, Jacksonville, Moline, and Peoria sent delegations to Springfield to express their desire for municipal rate regulation. From Chicago, Mayor Dunne and a committee of fifty prominent Chicagoans testified on the need for municipal regulation. The local delegations expressed unanimous opposition to state regulation. For example, Peoria's legal counsel argued that "a state commission would not be sufficiently in touch with local conditions."[4]

A Legislative History of the Enabling Act of 1905

In May 1905, the Illinois legislature passed the Enabling Act. The law empowered the Chicago City Council to regulate gas and electric rates. It also allowed the city to sell surplus gas and electricity. The Enabling Act grew out of three separate bills. First, house bill 644 (HB 644) enabled Illinois cities and towns to regulate gas and electric rates. The press called it the "state regulator bill." Second, house bill 683 (HB 683) enabled the City of Chicago to sell surplus gas and electricity. The press called it the "Chicago municipal ownership bill." Third, house bill 664 (HB 664) enabled the Chicago City Council (and no other Illinois towns) to regulate gas and electric rates. The press called it the "Chicago regulator bill." As passed, the Enabling Act combined the two Chicago measures, HB 664 and HB 683. The senate defeated the statewide version of the enabling bill, the state regulator bill.

Table 1 summarizes the legislative history of the Enabling Act. Four of the events call for additional comment. First, on April 19, the house referred the state regulator bill to the municipal corporations committee. The referral gave Illinois gas companies the chance to testify against enabling legislation. Supporters of the bill claimed that the gas lobby pushed for the referral to kill the bill. If the gas companies could keep the bill in committee long enough, the house would adjourn (in early May) before the floor had an opportunity to vote on it.

Second, on April 27, the state regulator bill emerged from committee, and the house set aside the Chicago regulator bill. According to the press, the house set aside the Chicago measure to appease representatives who served constituencies outside Chicago. Many of these legislators opposed laws that granted Chicago privileges not available to other municipalities in the state.

Third, on May 1, Representative Pederson, the chair of a key committee, forestalled a vote on the state regulator bill. Observers considered the delay serious. Because it was so late in the legislative session, the house could adjourn before it had a chance to vote on the bill.

Finally, on May 6, the senate passed the Enabling Act by a unanimous vote. The Enabling Act was an amended version of Chicago's municipal ownership bill. The act revived Chicago's original regulator bill by attaching it, as an amendment, to the municipal ownership bill. Like the senate, the house voted unanimously, 116 to 0, to pass the Enabling Act.[5]

The Enabling Act passed despite last-minute lobbying by Chicago gas companies. On the dawn of the act's passage, the *Tribune* (May 7, 1905, 4) reported:

> Early this morning, shortly after midnight, representatives of the gas interests were hustling around Springfield trying to line up enough men to defeat Chicago's bill [the Enabling Act]. Representatives were dragged out of bed. Others were found in back rooms of saloons, and others dragged away from poker games. Cabs were jumping all over downtown streets and every inducement that could be brought to bear was used to get a stone wall erected in front of the measure.

In contrast, Chicago voters overwhelmingly supported the Enabling Act. After it passed the state legislature, state law required that the city ratify

TABLE 1. The Enabling Act of 1905: A Legislative Overview

Date	Event
4/12	Representative introduced state regulator bill (HB 644).
4/19	State regulator bill referred to municipal corporations committee. Also, Chicago municipal ownership bill (HB 683) and Chicago regulator bill (HB 664) were introduced.
4/24	Downstate representatives withdrew opposition to Chicago regulator bill.
4/25	Chicago regulator bill (HB 664) emerged from the charter committee.
4/27	State regulator bill (HB 644) emerged from committee.
4/28	An amended version of the Chicago municipal ownership bill (HB 683) emerged from the charter committee.
5/1	Rep. Pederson blocked a vote on state regulator bill (HB 644).
5/2	House passed the state regulator bill (HB 644).
5/3	House passed Chicago's municipal ownership bill (HB 683).
5/4	Opposition senators announced they had enough votes to defeat the state bill (HB 644).
5/5	Senate defeated state regulator bill (HB 644).
5/6	Senate passed an amended version of the Chicago municipal ownership bill (HB 683); the amendment was the Chicago regulator bill (HB 664).
5/18	Governor Deneen signed bill into law.

the act in a local referendum. It passed by a decisive margin: 124,545 Chicagoans voted in favor of the law; 20,504 voted against it (*Chicago Tribune,* November 8, 1905, 1).

Passage of the Enabling Act: Implications and Qualifications

As I explained in chapter 2, Chicago gas producers could not easily redeploy their capital. Consequently, when Chicago gas producers first invested in the city, they demanded commitments that local authorities would not behave opportunistically ex post. A complex institutional nexus—a combination of state and federal constitutions, contracts, reputation, and so forth—embodied and supported these commitments. The passage of the Enabling Act degraded a *part* of this institutional nexus. It eliminated the constitutional prohibition against municipal regulation. Local authorities would now find it *less difficult* to engage in the political opportunism described in chapter 2.

A tension between notions of credible commitment and notions of institutional malleability manifests itself here. If the constitutional provision forestalling municipal rate regulation could be changed—all Chicago politicians had to do was lobby the legislature—how credible was the constitution to begin with? Or, more generally, if the institutions supporting credible commitment are subject to change over time, why would individuals accept them as credible in the first place? The answer is a matter of degree. In the long run, all institutions are subject to change, some more so than others. The original logic still applies. By forcing local governments to ask a third party, in this case, the state legislature, for the authority to regulate rates, the constitution made it more difficult for local politicians to pursue overzealous regulatory policies. Beyond this, the Enabling Act did not undermine all the institutions preventing the city from behaving opportunistically. Other institutional constraints, such as substantive due process, remained viable. The viability of these other institutions motivates my use of the words *part* and *less difficult:* because *part* of the original institutional nexus remained, local politicians merely found it *less difficult* to behave opportunistically; they were still not completely free of constraints on their behavior.

An Event Study of the Enabling Act

If investors believed that municipal regulation promoted lower gas rates, and lower profits, the market value of Chicago gas companies would have fallen with passage of the Enabling Act. Alternatively, if investors believed that municipal regulation promoted higher gas rates, and higher profits, the market value of Chicago gas companies would have risen with the act's passage.

I use an event study to identify how the stock price of the Peoples Gas Light and Coke Company reacted to the passage of the Enabling Act. Returns for the company are calculated using daily closing price data collected from the *New York Times*. Returns on the market are calculated using the Dow Jones index. The data consist of forty-six observations. They end five trading days before the first event described in table 1. Using these data, I estimate an out-of-sample model. I then use the parameter estimates from this model to predict the normal rate of return on days during the sample period, the period during which the Enabling Act was passed. Subtracting predicted or normal returns from realized returns yields an estimate of excess returns. Presumably, excess returns will be negative on those days when adverse events took place and positive on those days when positive events occurred. The cumulative excess return on any given event day is the summation of all previous days' excess returns. (See app. B for more details.)

To estimate normal returns, I regress the variable CHI_t against MKT_t, MKT_{t-1} and MKT_{t+1}. CHI_t is the realized daily rate of return for the Peoples Gas Light and Coke Company on day t. MKT_t is the realized daily rate of return on the market portfolio on day t. MKT_{t-1} and MKT_{t+1} are the realized daily rate of return on the market portfolio for day t lagged by one day and led by one day. Following Dimson (1979), I include the lagged and led market return terms to control for the possibility of non-synchronous trading.

Figure 4 plots the cumulative excess returns associated with passage of the Enabling Act of 1905. The path of cumulative excess returns squares well with the preceding analysis. It suggests that the senate's passage of the Enabling Act reduced the value of Chicago gas securities by roughly 10 percent. Also, on May 5, 1905, the day the senate defeated the statewide regulator bill, cumulative excess returns jumped about 5 percent. Similarly, the days following the passage of the Enabling Act were associated with large negative excess returns. Finally, note the steady upward drift in cumulative returns after May 18. Rumors that the Enabling Act was unconstitutional may have contributed to this upward drift.[6]

Voting Patterns on the Statewide Enabling Bill

As already noted, if there were substantial political risk associated with municipal rate regulation, legislators representing districts with limited gas service would have been less likely to vote in favor of the statewide

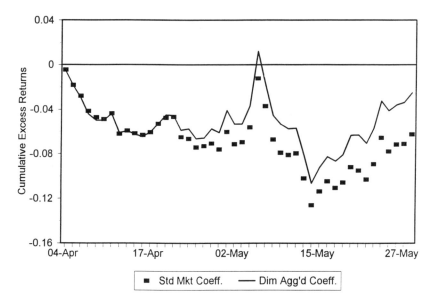

Fig. 4. Excess returns associated with passage of the Enabling Act of 1905

enabling bill (HB 644). The underlying intuition is straightforward. Regions without a gas company, or with only limited gas service, would have opposed the law because it made it difficult for them to credibly commit to nonconfiscatory policies. In turn, the inability to credibly commit would have discouraged entrepreneurs from investing in gas production and distribution capital; entrepreneurs would have feared the imposition of onerous regulations after they made their investments. If, however, the region did not possess the authority to regulate rates, local authorities would have been constrained from behaving opportunistically. This would have protected new investments from confiscatory policies and helped attract gas production and distribution capital to the area. Employing the same logic, regions with a substantial level of gas production would have been less likely to oppose municipal rate regulation.

To test this argument, I use the following data. First, I calculate per capita gas production for each of Illinois's fifty-one legislative districts in 1904. I identify the location of each district with maps from the *Illinois Apportionment Handbook* (1911). The *Handbook* also shows population levels for each district. Using the 1906 *Brown's Directory of American Gas Companies,* I gather production data for every gas company in Illinois. Using a map, I then place the gas companies in their respective electoral districts and calculate total district gas production. Lastly, I exclude from the analysis all representatives whose party affiliation or district I could not identify.

With these data, I estimate a probit model for the two house votes and one senate vote on the statewide enabling bill. I regress the variable $VOTE_i$ against $PARTY_i$, GAS_i, and $PARTY*GAS_i$. $VOTE_i$ is a dummy variable that identifies how the legislator voted. A 1 indicates a yes vote; a 0 indicates a no vote. (Following convention, I exclude abstentions from the analysis.) $PARTY_i$ is a dummy variable that identifies party affiliation: a 1 indicates a Democrat; a 0 indicates a Republican. GAS_i is per capita gas production in the legislator's district. $PARTY*GAS_i$ is an interaction term that controls for the possibility that the effects of per capita gas consumption differed across party.

Table 2 summarizes the votes considered and identifies the predicted sign on *GAS,* per capita gas production. Consider first the house vote referring the state regulator bill to the municipal corporations committee. Recall that supporters of the state regulator bill claimed that the referral was intended to kill the measure. If the preceding argument is correct, legislators representing regions with negligible amounts of gas production would have favored the referral. The vote to refer was a voice vote and as a result went unrecorded by the state congressional reporter. However, a reporter from the *Chicago Tribune* (April 20, 1905, 1–2) who was present for the vote managed to record a small sample of the legislators voting on the bill. The second vote considered is the house vote on the state bill. The same reasoning leads me to predict that legislators from districts with relatively high levels of per capita gas production would have been more likely to vote in favor of the statewide enabling bill. The third vote considered is the senate vote on the state bill. The same logic applies.

Table 3 describes the data used in each regression. Note that the value of *GAS* is expressed in thousands of cubic feet (MCF); per capita gas production varies from 0 to 6,760 cubic feet of gas per person. Table 4 reports the regression results. Table 5 reports the matrices of predicted and actual votes. For each vote, after controlling for the effects of party, the variable

TABLE 2. Votes Analyzed and Predicted Signs

VOTE	Description of Vote
(1)	House vote to refer state regulator bill (HB 644) to committee. Observers considered a yes vote equivalent to a vote in favor of killing the bill. (–)[a]
(2)	House vote passing state regular bill. (+)[a]
(3)	Senate vote defeating the state regulator bill. (+)[a]

[a] Predicted sign on *GAS,* per capita gas production.

GAS is significant and has the predicted sign. Regions that had relatively low (high) levels of gas consumption opposed (favored) expanding the regulatory power of municipal authorities. These results may help explain why the Chicago-specific enabling bill passed while the statewide enabling bill did not. Perhaps Chicago gas producers had completed (or nearly completed) their main system while producers in other Illinois cities had

TABLE 3.   Descriptive Statistics

	House Vote to Commit (1)	House Vote State-Wide Bill (2)	Senate Vote State-Wide Bill (3)
N	43	107	39
VOTE, number of obs. equal to 1	25	92	23
PARTY, number of obs. equal to 1	9	35	4
GAS[a]			
mean	3.94	3.53	3.14
max.	6.76	6.76	6.76
min.	0.00	0.00	0.00
std. dev.	3.01	3.01	3.05

[a]Gas production per capita is in thousands of cubic feet (MCF) per person.

TABLE 4.   Regression Results

Variable	House Vote to Commit (1)	House Vote State Bill (2)	Senate Vote State Bill (3)
VOTE (dependent variable)			
CONSTANT	1.924	0.302	−0.567
	(3.196)**	(1.282)	(1.801)*
PARTY	−1.104	1.249	6.172
	(1.135)	(1.974)*	(0.008)
GAS	−0.377	0.220	0.236
	(3.599)**	(2.899)*	(2.912)**
*GAS*PARTY*	0.214	−0.088	−0.236
	(1.192)	(0.429)	(0.148)
N	43	107	39
Likelihood Ratio Test	19.654	18.173	14.037

Note: asymptotic *t*-values are in parentheses.
*Significant at the .05 level.
**Significant at the .01 level.

not. A subsequent section of this chapter, "The Timing of Municipal Rate Regulation," presents evidence consistent with this hypothesis. Note that the results on the senate vote (table 4 (3)) suggest some degree of collinearity. I reran all of the regressions (table 4 (1–3)) excluding the interaction term. The collinearity disappears, but the other results remain the same. Legislators from areas with low per capita gas production tended to oppose the statewide version of the enabling bill.

Based on the regressions in table 4, table 6 provides measures of how large changes in gas production affected voting patterns. Holding party constant, table 6 compares the voting behavior of a legislator from Chicago (an area with a well-developed gas industry) to the voting behavior of a legislator from Pontiac, Illinois (an area with a poorly developed gas industry). The table shows, for example, that a Pontiac Republican would have been three times more likely than a Chicago Republican to vote in favor of committing (or killing) the bill. Similarly, a Republican senator from Pontiac would have been half as likely as a Chicago senator to vote in favor of the bill. Table 6 also suggests that *GAS* had a much smaller effect on the voting behavior of Democrats.

TABLE 5. Matrices of Predicted and Actual Votes

| | | Actual Votes | | | | | |
| | | Vote to Commit (1) | | House Vote (2) | | Senate Vote (3) | |
		0(NO)	1(YES)	0(NO)	1(YES)	0(NO)	1(YES)
Predicted Votes	0(NO)	16	7	0	0	13	7
	1(YES)	2	18	15	92	3	16

TABLE 6. How the Level of per Capita Gas Production Affected Voting Patterns

	House Vote to Commit (1)	House Vote State-Wide Bill (2)	Senate Vote State-Wide Bill (3)
The probability of a Republican from:			
Chicago (*GAS* = 6.76)	0.27	0.96	0.85
Pontiac (*GAS* = 0.10)	0.97	0.63	0.29
voting yes on 1, 2, or 3			
The probability of a Democrat from:			
Chicago (*GAS* = 6.76)	0.39	0.99	1.00
Pontiac (*GAS* = 0.10)	0.79	0.95	1.00
voting yes on 1, 2, or 3			

The Politics of Local Rate Regulation, Part I

In November 1905, shortly after passage of the Enabling Act, Mayor Edward Dunne submitted to the city council an ordinance reducing gas rates to 75 cents. Understanding what happened to Dunne's ordinance requires a little background. In 1905, two competing factions dominated the Chicago Democratic Party. Roger Sullivan of the Ogden Gas Company controlled one faction; Carter Harrison controlled the other. Mayor Dunne, though a Democrat, belonged to neither the Harrison nor the Sullivan faction. Dunne was elected mayor on a reform platform and the promise of "IMO" or immediate municipal ownership of the city's traction system.[7]

Mayor Dunne did not enjoy the undivided support of his party. Only about one-third of all Democratic aldermen supported him regularly. Many of Harrison's supporters resented Dunne from the start because of his outspoken and harsh criticism of Harrison's traction policies. Sullivan's people came to dislike Dunne when he began removing their supporters and friends from patronage jobs. Add to this the fact that Republicans controlled the city council during his term, and you begin to see why one biographer said that Dunne's "mayoralty turned out to be the most frustrating period of his life."[8]

Legislatively, Dunne could accomplish little without the support of the city council, and the council stonewalled him every chance it got. For example, Dunne tried to appoint John F. Finerty to the board of local improvements in December 1905. By all accounts, this was a trivial matter. The city council, however, refused to confirm Finerty. This was the first time in the city's history that the council blocked a mayoral appointment. On more substantive matters, the council blocked Dunne's municipal ownership program and his efforts to reduce electric rates to levels he thought reasonable.[9]

The city council's unwillingness to work with Dunne shaped the battle over gas rates. When Dunne introduced his 75-cent ordinance, several key members of the city council balked. They refused to pass the ordinance without first investigating the costs of manufacturing and distributing gas. The mayor retorted that 75 cents was a reasonable rate and that gas companies were obligated to show otherwise. There was no need for a lengthy and costly investigation. The mayor buttressed his claims by pointing to Cincinnati and Wheeling (West Virginia) where gas sold for 75 cents. Still the council refused to go along with the mayor. It would take up the gas question in its own way and in its own time.[10]

While the city council dismissed the mayor's rumblings for 75-cent gas, gas companies took them seriously. The Peoples Gas Company filed papers in federal court, claiming that the Enabling Act was unconstitutional. The company also offered the city a compromise. It would reduce its rate from $1 to 90 cents. The company maintained that it could not sell gas at a rate of less than 90 cents and make a profit. To bolster its claim, Peoples Gas cut its dividend rate from 6 to 5 percent and explained to its stockholders that "the directors decided to reduce the dividend rate to a 5 percent basis, made necessary by the offer to reduce the price of gas to 90 cents." It was a cheap ploy. A short time later, the company would consent to an 85-cent rate and return its dividend rate to 6 percent. Finally, the company challenged Mayor Dunne's comparison of Chicago with Cincinnati and Wheeling. James Meagher, the legal counsel for Peoples Gas, argued:

> You were told that gas is sold for 75 cents in Wheeling, but you were not told the deficit for the last three years there has been $20,000 a year. You were told the rate in Cincinnati is 75 cents but you were not told that the best gas making coal, which comes from Pennsylvania—we can't make gas from our Illinois coal—is shot down a chute from the mine into a barge which is floated down the Ohio river and tied up to the yards of the gas works in Cincinnati.[11]

On December 6, 1905, the city council decided to move ahead with an investigation of the costs of manufacturing and distributing gas. The mayor wanted the council to hire Edward W. Bemis to investigate gas rates. Bemis, a former professor of political economy at the University of Chicago, shared Mayor Dunne's conviction that utilities should be municipally owned. Bemis also had a history of denouncing the high prices charged by Chicago gas companies. In an interview with the *Chicago Daily Leader* in 1895, Bemis declared that gas in Chicago should sell for 55 cents. At the time, gas sold for $1.10. In 1896, the Illinois Bureau of Labor Statistics hired Bemis to write a detailed study of the Chicago gas industry. In that report, Bemis wrote: "every evidence seems to indicate that in Chicago all charges for gas above 50 cents and possibly above 45 cents are profit."[12]

Council members agreed to hire Bemis but only if they could also hire two other experts of their own choosing, E. G. Cowdery and Alexander C. Humphreys. When he testified, Cowdery was president of the LaClede Gas Company in St. Louis. Within two years, he would become the vice president of the Peoples Gas Light and Coke Company. Within ten years, he would become the company's president. Humphreys came to the city highly recommended. The *Chicago Tribune* called him the "best expert on gas in the country." Bemis recommended Humphreys to the council as "the leading authority in the world on gas." Humphreys was president of the Stevens Institute of Technology, a technical school in New Jersey. He was also president of the Buffalo Gas Company. No one had to worry that Cowdery and Humphreys would reveal any prejudice against Chicago gas companies. If council members wanted their experts to undercut Dunne's expert, they chose well.[13]

None of the city's consultants—not Bemis, Cowdery, or Humphreys—performed a detailed investigation of the companies' books and plant, as was standard practice. City authorities only asked that the experts review conditions in Chicago. Bemis and Humphreys expressed surprise and discomfort at this. Asked to give testimony on his first day in Chicago, Bemis said: "I have never appeared in a gas case in which I was expected to give information the first day I was in the case." Similarly, Humphreys said: "I must say at the outset that it has not been my practice to give advice . . . without a thorough examination. I have not had the opportunity to make such an examination here, nor would I have within the limits that you have set as to time."[14]

Whatever their qualms, Cowdery and Humphreys both recommended a 95-cent rate. Both men also encouraged the city to accept the 90-cent compromise offered by Peoples Gas. Bemis disagreed, recommending a 75-cent rate as more than sufficient. In a letter to Mayor Dunne, Bemis maintained that gas companies could charge 65 cents and still make a profit. Asked by one councilman if the city should compromise and agree to a rate greater than 75 cents, Bemis was indignant: "I would not advise any kind of a compromise. The city should fight for its rights until it gets them. Seventy-five cents is a reasonable price for gas in Chicago under present conditions."[15]

Mayor Dunne and Bemis wanted a 75-cent rate. Cowdery and Humphreys wanted a 95-cent rate. The council split the difference. By a vote of 58 to 9, the city council passed an ordinance setting gas rates at 85 cents for five years. The council included two givebacks in the 85-cent ordinance. First, the ordinance did not require gas companies to compensate the city for the use of the streets. Earlier ordinances often required producers to pay the city a percentage of their earnings as compensation. Second, the ordinance repealed provisions in the franchises of the Ogden and Universal gas companies that prohibited them from leasing or selling their property to the Peoples Gas Company. Although Peoples Gas had been colluding with both companies for several years, this new ordinance paved the way for their formal acquisition. (See chap. 5 for more details on the acquisition.)[16]

The council's 85-cent ordinance required a 15 percent reduction in gas rates. This was the largest single-year reduction in gas rates since the early 1880s. Despite its tendency to smite the mayor at every turn, the city council felt compelled to pass an ordinance with at least a few teeth in it.

Mayor Dunne threatened to veto the 85-cent ordinance and pass an even stronger measure. Only if the gas companies accepted three conditions would he allow the 85-cent ordinance to become law. First, Dunne asked that gas companies not charge the city for gas used in street lighting. Second, he asked that the city receive a fixed percentage of the companies' earnings. Third, the mayor wanted the rate to be set for three years, not five, as prescribed by the council's ordinance. The gas companies refused the offer. They were not even sure if they would acquiesce to the 85-cent rate. The mayor made good on part of his threat. On February 13, he vetoed the 85-cent ordinance. The next day, however, the city council overrode his veto and passed the ordinance. This was the first time in nearly a decade that the council had overridden a mayoral veto. A day later, local gas companies backed down and accepted the 85-cent rate. Why producers acquiesced is not clear. Perhaps the risk of a long and expensive legal battle and the city's givebacks combined to make the 85-cent ordinance attractive.[17]

Even under the best conditions, setting gas rates was not an exact science. Interpretation and chance always played a role. In 1906, Chicago authorities pushed interpretation and chance too far. Before any investigation, Mayor Dunne wanted 75-cent gas. The city council thwarted Dunne but not because it felt obligated to seriously investigate gas rates. The council's own investigation was not that serious. The council hired three consultants, none of whom appeared especially impartial or unbiased. Before arriving in the city, Bemis was partial to Dunne's position. After his arrival, Cowdery became very partial to the gas company's position. Lacking prejudice, the council's investigation would still fall short. Bemis and Humphreys admitted that the city's time constraints prevented them from performing complete investigations. But forget the prejudice and the hurried analysis. The council fixed an 85-cent rate because it was halfway between the rate recommended by Bemis and the rate recommended by Cowdery and Humphreys. Why go halfway? Why not give Bemis's recommendation more weight because Peoples Gas enjoyed a monopoly for so many years? Why not give Humphreys' recommendation more weight because he, according to Bemis, was the world's greatest gas expert?

The Politics of Local Rate Regulation, Part II

On December 1, 1910, several months before the 85-cent ordinance was set to expire, Alderman Herman Bauler and several other Chicago politicians incorporated the 70 Cent Gas League. Bauler explained that the Gas League planned to call on every city council candidate to sign a pledge to 70-cent gas. If a candidate refused to sign, Bauler promised to use it against the candidate in the upcoming election. Seventy-cent gas resonated with broad cross sections of the population. Local businesses supported the Gas League along with women's groups. Chicago politicians responded. Of the thirty-seven Democrats running for the city council, twenty-five signed the pledge. Of the thirty-seven Republicans running, twenty-two signed.[18]

The 70 Cent League did not affect the Republican mayoral primary. Alderman Charles Merriam refused to sign on to 70-cent gas and won the primary with ease. Merriam refused to sign because he was the chair of the city council's committee investigating gas rates.

The 70 Cent League did affect the Democratic primary. Abandoning his 1900 claim that regulating rates would let politicians "blackmail" gas companies, candidate Carter Harrison pledged himself to 70-cent gas. Harrison faced two opponents in the primary: Edward Dunne, who had lost his bid for reelection in 1907, and Andrew J. Graham. Dunne again ran as a reformer. He did not make 70-cent gas the centerpiece of his campaign as did Harrison, but after 1906 his commitment to low gas rates spoke for itself. Roger Sullivan backed the third candidate, Andrew Graham. In contrast to Harrison and Dunne, Graham refused to commit himself to any rate. He publicly condemned the Gas League.[19]

Little more than a mouthpiece for Roger Sullivan, Graham spoke presciently nonetheless. In one speech, he argued that "to make gas . . . or other rates footballs of party or factional politics is to make honest government and honest service of the public difficult, if not utterly impossible." "Clamor and guess work," he went on, "may suit office seekers, but they do not promote industry." He concluded: "Nothing would be easier than to achieve a cheap and transient popularity than by yielding to an uninformed clamor for a particular price for a particular commodity." Graham was right: nothing was easier. Harrison won the Democratic primary. Dunne was a close second, and Graham came in a distant third. Graham might have been an astute political observer, but he was no politician.[20]

Harrison, on the other hand, knew a good thing when he saw it. During the general election he again made 70-cent gas the centerpiece of his campaign. Merriam's campaign focused on municipal reform and cleaning up city hall. As in the primary, he refused to sign the 70-cent pledge. Harrison turned Merriam's refusal to sign the 70-cent pledge into something sinister. In speech after speech, the Harrison campaign reiterated its commitment to 70-cent gas, while attributing the worst possible motives to Merriam. "I would like to know," one Harrison supporter chided, "if Ald. Merriam will inform the public about the agreement . . . between himself and the various public utility corporations under which he receives their support, chiefly financial, for his campaign. What is to be their reward?"[21]

During the campaign, party affiliation meant little. Dunne vacationed in Michigan, damning Harrison with silence. Roger Sullivan was more direct. In his autobiography, Harold Ickes, Merriam's campaign manager, relates how Sullivan met and shared with him the best ways to defeat Harrison. After the election, Merriam acknowledged that the Sullivan faction had supported him but said that he had in no way agreed to that support. On the Republican side, many party regulars worked against Merriam or gave him only faint support.[22]

It was a close race. Carter Harrison won by seventeen thousand votes. For the fifth and final time in his life, he would serve as Chicago's mayor. Harrison, unlike Graham and Merriam, was a career politician. Graham was a banker. Merriam was a political science professor at the University of Chicago and had only recently won his aldermanic seat.

Edward Kantowicz calls Harrison's 1911 campaign "a model of successful progressive politics" for a city like Chicago. He identifies three central features of the campaign. First, as a Democrat, Harrison had the right party affiliation for a city with a large immigrant population. Second, Harrison "played skillfully on the nationalistic loyalties of Chicago's immigrant population." Third, "seventy-cent gas gave Harrison a specific, easily understood issue he could sell in every ward of the city."[23]

Harrison affirmed his commitment to 70-cent gas on the day he was elected. When a *Tribune* reporter asked the new mayor what subject was of "prime importance" for his upcoming administration, he responded that it was "a conservative and uniform policy regarding public utilities and construction of a Chicago subway." The stock market believed Harrison's promise to deliver low gas rates. The *Commercial and Financial Chronicle* reported that the stock price of Peoples Gas "declined sharply" following the election. A formal event study suggests that the market value of Peoples Gas fell by nearly 5 percent on election day.[24]

In the fall of 1910, months before the election, the city hired W. J. Hagenah to head an investigation into the costs of manufacturing and distributing coal gas in Chicago. Hagenah, chief accountant of Wisconsin's utilities commission, spent six months investigating the company's plants and books. Several engineers and accountants associated with the Wisconsin utilities commission helped in the investigation. Hagenah promised that he and his colleagues at the Wisconsin commission would perform a thorough and careful investigation:

It is a problem of tremendous importance. It is the largest gas investigation in the history of the world. Every large city in this country is interested greatly in its conclusion. It may wind up in the highest courts of the country. I am desirous from the most selfish reasons to present to this [council] the most complete and thorough report which I can possibly prepare. I want it to be my best effort, something I can point to with pride.[25]

Hagenah presented his report to the city council in mid-April, shortly after the election. He recommended that the price of gas be set at 77 cents. Hagenah said that 77 cents was the lowest rate he could recommend and still allow producers a reasonable return. He went on to say that "the attempt to fix even that rate may result in litigation." The Peoples Gas Light and Coke Company agreed. Calling the 77-cent rate "ridiculous and impossible," the company promised to litigate if the council enacted the rate.[26]

Members of the city council also found the 77-cent rate less than satisfactory but for a different reason: many of them had promised their constituents a 70-cent rate. The city council tabled Hagenah's report, introduced an ordinance reducing gas rates to 70 cents, and began searching for a new expert. According to the *Tribune,* council members hoped that this new expert would "whittle the price lower than 77 cents." The city hired Edward Bemis. Bemis had recommended a 75-cent rate during the city's 1906 investigation. Bemis's appointment thrilled the *Chicago Examiner,* a local paper whose editorial policy stood foursquare behind the demand for 70-cent gas. The *Examiner* proclaimed: "Bemis is the kind of expert who does not stand in awe of the bookkeeping methods of gas corporation[s]." The paper continued: "Unlike Hagenah, he approaches the subject without any regard to what the gas company's ledgers say the plant is worth, or what it would cost to duplicate."[27]

It did not really matter if Bemis approached the subject "without any regard" for what the company's ledgers said. Peoples Gas refused to cooperate with the new investigation and denied Bemis the right to examine its books. In a letter to the city, the company cited two reasons for its refusal. First, the letter claimed that several members of the city council, as well as Mayor Harrison, had pledged themselves to 70-cent gas; no matter what the investigation said, the city would go ahead and pass a 70-cent ordinance. Second, the letter claimed that Bemis held a prejudice against the company; no matter what the company's books said, Bemis would recommend a 70-cent rate.[28]

Without access to the company's books, Bemis could not do his own independent evaluation of Chicago's situation. Instead, he reviewed

Hagenah's report for errors. Bemis found no areas where he thought Hagenah had been too hard on the gas company. He did, however, find several areas where he thought Hagenah had been too generous to the company. Hagenah, for example, allowed the company a 7 percent rate of return. Bemis thought a 6 percent return more appropriate. Hagenah accepted the company's accounting when it claimed it had purchased 900 million cubic feet of gas at 50 cents (per MCF) from the Northwestern Gas Light and Coke Company. Bemis rejected it, arguing that the company could have manufactured the gas itself for about half the price.[29]

In his report, Bemis concluded that the city council could fix the price of gas at 66 cents and still allow the company a reasonable return. He wrote, however, that "the case for the city could be made even stronger" if the city adopted the following five-year rate schedule: 75 cents for the rest of 1911; 70 cents for 1912, 1913, and 1914; and 65 cents for 1915. Still, the city council was not completely satisfied. According to the *Chicago Record-Herald,* Bemis had to "revise" his calculations so that they "conformed" with the ideas of the council. With this, Hagenah erupted. In "a stormy scene" he resigned, declaring that he was "tired of being a football for a crowd of politicians." In the end, the city council passed an ordinance close to the one recommended by Bemis. It set rates at 75 cents for the rest of 1911, 70 cents for the next two years, and 68 cents for the last two years.[30]

The Peoples Gas Light and Coke Company claimed that the ordinance was arbitrary and confiscatory. It refused to lower its rate from 85 cents and appealed to the courts for injunctive relief. In August 1911, a circuit court judge, Judge Gibbons, fixed gas rates at 80 cents pending further litigation. The city responded, filing its own suit in the same circuit court but before a different judge. The city asked that the court direct the gas company "to pay over to the clerk of the court . . . all moneys collected from consumers, in excess of the maximum rates prescribed by such ordinance." The court sided with the city and issued a mandatory injunction impounding the difference between the 80-cent rate and the rates dictated by the 70-cent ordinance.[31]

The Peoples Gas Company appealed to an Illinois appellate court and filed a second independent suit in federal court. On appeal, the appellate court reversed the circuit court's order. The company continued charging 80 cents. The appellate court explained that the lower court was empowered to grant the city's impounding order only in cases of "extreme urgency, where the right is clear indeed and free from reasonable doubt." The "obvious question" confronted by the court was "whether such an extreme case [was] made by the bill and exhibits in this case." The court found that the bill and exhibits did not make such an extreme case:

In view of the facts that the city employed two experts in succession to assist in its determination of the reasonable rate to be fixed by ordinance; that these experts disagreed in their conclusions; that the report of the first (which was the result of six months' investigation of the properties, books and papers of the defendant) recommended a higher rate than the ordinance prescribes; that the second report was based upon an analysis of the first, with little, if any, independent examination of the facts, and that all these matters are alleged by the city in its bill of complaint, it certainly cannot be said that the case thus presented is so very clear and so free from reasonable doubt as to come within the class of cases in which the trial court is justified in granting to a complainant in advance of a hearing upon the merits this exceptional and extraordinary process.[32]

Two court decisions, one in 1918 and the other in 1927, finally resolved the dispute between the city and Peoples Gas. In 1918, the Illinois Supreme Court declared the Enabling Act unconstitutional. The court called the act a "clear and palpable violation" of the Illinois constitutional provision that no law embrace more than one subject—the Enabling Act allowed the city to regulate rates *and* sell surplus gas and electricity. In 1927, the court built on its earlier decision and ruled that Peoples Gas did not have to refund money to Chicago consumers for having refused to obey the 70-cent ordinance.[33]

That the courts eventually declared the Enabling Act unconstitutional does not undermine its historical significance. The act produced two local rate ordinances, one cut gas rates by 15 percent and the other, if enforced, would have cut rates by nearly 20 percent. The legal battle over the second ordinance lasted nearly two decades, involved the state and federal courts, and was twice carried to the Illinois Supreme Court. The Enabling Act's most enduring legacy, however, was that it helped define the political battle over state utility regulation a few years later. (Chapter 7 discusses the origins of state regulation.)

Edward Webster Bemis and the Market for Experts

Chicago authorities paid a premium for Bemis's expert advice. Bemis charged the city sixty-five dollars per day; Hagenah charged the city fifty dollars a day. Bemis usually charged the city for holidays and Sundays; Hagenah did not. Bemis charged the city about $2,500 for his services on gas. In current dollars, Bemis charged the city more than $35,000 for a month's time. Hagenah's monthly rate was less than one-fifth Bemis's rate. Despite high fees, Bemis remained a very popular utility expert. His work on gas rates so pleased Chicago authorities that they hired him to investigate the city's telephone rates a short time later. By the fall of 1911, local authorities in Des Moines, Iowa, and Omaha, Nebraska, had hired Bemis to investigate gas rates in their cities.[34]

Bemis had one explanation for the premium cities put on his services. Holmgren writes: "Bemis assumed from the numerous demands for his presence at investigations that he was the only independent expert on gas and electric utilities in the country." Holmgren draws this conclusion from a newspaper interview in which Bemis said, "It appears to me that the rest [of the experts] are nearly all of them tied up to the corporations. The number of calls I have received of late causes me to believe that my position has become rather monopolistic, as I seem to have the field to myself." It is possible that every other gas expert in the country was a corporate advocate. Of course, even if corporate ties tainted some or even most other experts that does not preclude the possibility that Bemis also acted as an advocate. In a Ph.D. dissertation expressly sympathetic to Bemis, Holmgren (1964) writes that Bemis's "convictions impelled him to align himself with the cities in franchise negotiations and rate cases."[35]

The Timing of Municipal Rate Regulation

The passage of the Enabling Act and Carter Harrison's campaign for 70-cent gas a few years later coincided with two other changes. First, by the early twentieth century, the electric industry began to expand rapidly. Chicago's primary electric provider, the Commonwealth Edison Company, generated fifteen times more electricity in 1910 than it had in 1900. The development of the electric industry may have encouraged Chicago authorities to adopt harsher regulatory policies toward local gas companies. If politicians believed that the completion of the city's electrical network meant certain death for gas lighting they may have been less concerned about adopting overzealous regulatory policies. Who would have cared if they set gas prices so low that gas companies stopped investing? Consumers who were unable to find gas for lighting simply would have purchased electricity.[36]

A second potentially important change was a slowdown in the growth of Chicago's gas system when measured in per capita main mileage. To see why this may have been important consider the following logic. Chicago's population imposed a natural ceiling on the number of mains producers could have installed in the city; in any given year, there were only so many homes and businesses that wanted gas. As long as producers were below this natural ceiling (i.e., plenty of the city's current residents demanded gas but could not purchase it because their neighborhoods were not piped), the number of gas mains installed in the city would have been growing at a faster rate than the population. When below the ceiling, not only did producers have to install mains to provide service to newly arrived residents of the city, they also had to install mains to provide service to the indigenous residents of the city who were without gas service. Crudely put, producers would have been playing catchup. Once producers caught up (i.e., none of the city's indigenous population that demanded gas service was without such service), any new main construction would have been dedicated solely to providing service to newly arrived residents of the city; that is, the number of new gas mains installed every year would have just kept pace with increases in the population.

In short, when the number of gas mains per capita was increasing over time, this implies that a substantial portion of Chicago's (current or indigenous) population was without gas service. Alternatively, when the number of gas mains per capita was stable over time, it suggests that most of the city's (indigenous) population had gas service if it wanted such service.

Figure 5 plots the total miles of gas mains in Chicago per thousand persons. The data used to construct figure 5 suggest that prior to 1900, per capita main mileage grew at a rate of 4 percent a year. After 1900, per capita main mileage grew at a rate of 0.1 percent a year. The data suggest that during the nineteenth century, large cross sections of Chicago's population wanted, but did not have, gas service. Growth in main mileage outran population growth, and per capita main mileage grew steadily; gas companies installed new mains to provide service for newly arrived residents and indigenous Chicagoans who were without gas service. By the early 1900s, however, it appears that the vast majority of the indigenous population that wanted gas service had such service. Growth in main mileage just kept pace with population growth, and per capita main mileage stabilized at 1.2 miles of mains per thousand persons. Gas companies installed new mains only for newly arrived residents.

Considering the stabilization of per capita main mileage during the early 1900s, one might think of the Enabling Act as part of a natural endgame strategy. When producers first began investing in the city in, say, 1860, the number of consumers who demanded but did not have gas service because their particular block was not piped far exceeded the number of consumers who demanded, and actually had, gas service. The number of people who wanted to encourage future investment was large. In this context, there would have been substantial political pressure on local regulators to avoid imposing onerous regulations on gas companies. If the city imposed onerous policies, gas producers would have refused to continue installing mains, leaving much of the city without gas service. Pre-

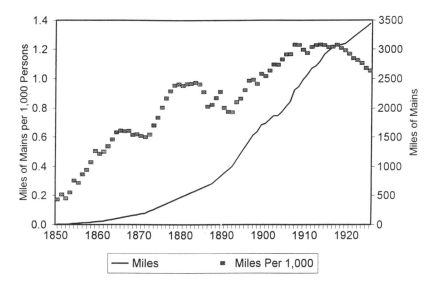

Fig. 5. Miles of gas mains per 1,000 persons, 1850–1924. (For miles of gas mains, see: Illinois Bureau of Labor Statistics [1897]; Andreas [1975], vol. 2, 702; Andreas [1975], vol. 3, 128; and the annual reports of the Peoples Gas Light and Coke Company, 1897–1925. For a few years, missing values are interpolated. For Chicago's population reported by year, see Hoyt [1933], 483.)

sumably, local politicians would have paid an electoral price for such a result. Consumers who wanted but could not purchase gas because their section of the city was not piped would have voted against politicians who discouraged development of the gas industry by promoting onerous policies. In contrast, during the early 1900s, when per capita main mileage stabilized, the number of consumers who demanded but did not have gas service because their particular city block was not piped was far less than the number of consumers who demanded, and actually had, gas service. The number of people concerned about promoting future investment was small. In this context, the political pressures to impose low rates on gas companies would have been much greater. Low rates would have won votes from current gas consumers and lost votes only among the few Chicagoans who wanted but were still without service.

Comparisons

In a speech before the Pacific Gas Association, an officer of a San Francisco gas company said the following:

>When the time for the regulation of rates arises, a [city] councilman or supervisor, elected on a platform that calls for a reduction in the gas and electric rates, is hardly in a proper frame of mind to listen to evidence and impartially vote thereon. No matter what the evidence is, if he does not vote for a reduction a large number of citizens, and all of the daily papers, will accuse him of being biased in favor of the corporation.[37]

In his history of the Wisconsin electric industry, Forrest McDonald writes: "At the turn of the century, public utilities were regulated by municipal governments. Such regulation was governed largely by political concerns; shrewd politicians . . . recognized . . . that voters were often inclined to respond favorably to attacks on utilities."[38]

As these quotations imply, local rate regulation in other cities worked much like it did in Chicago. Consider three examples. On May 4, 1891, the Cleveland City Council passed an ordinance requiring the city's two gas companies to reduce their rates from $1 to 60 cents. The ordinance grew out of a plan launched by Cleveland's newly elected mayor, who thought the city paid too much to light streets and public buildings. He directed several members of the city council to meet and devise a plan to lower the city's gas bill. At one of these meetings, one council member suggested that private consumers also paid too much for their gas. Someone else then said that the price of gas for private consumers should be reduced to 60 cents. Although no one explained why, the other council members present agreed that 60 cents was a good rate. Within a few days, an ordinance setting rates at 60 cents had been introduced and passed. One of the city's gas companies sued, requesting an injunction. After a year in court, neither the city nor the company saw the litigation ending soon. In the summer of 1892, the city and the gas companies resolved their differences and agreed to an 80-cent rate.[39]

In 1887, Tennessee passed a law empowering Memphis officials to regulate gas rates, subject to the provision that they never set rates below $1.50. A few years later, without any investigation into the costs of producing and distributing gas, the Memphis City Council ordered the New Memphis Gas Company to reduce its rates to $1.50. The company sued, claiming that the $1.50 rate was confiscatory. A federal court agreed and granted the company injunctive relief.[40]

The experience of Peoria, Illinois, not only highlights the politics of local rate regulation, it also speaks to the law and the dynamics of institutional change. As in Chicago, the efforts of Peoria gas companies to monopolize their industry provided the impetus for municipal regulation. As in Chicago, municipal rate regulation was arbitrary and politicized. As in Chicago, the courts blocked capricious regulations.

In 1899, Peoria authorities granted a franchise to the Peoria Gas and Electric Company. Until then, the Peoria Gaslight and Coke Company had dominated the city's gas market. The new company initiated a price war. By the early summer of 1900, gas prices in Peoria had fallen by 70 percent, from $1 to 30 cents. Then, in July 1900, immediately after a meeting between managers of the two companies, both companies raised their rates to $1.15. The increase in gas prices caused consumers to organize and protest. Local politicians responded. In August 1900, on a unanimous vote, the city council ordered gas companies to reduce their rates to 75 cents. Before ordering the rate reduction, the council had made no investigation into the costs of manufacturing and distributing gas. Although local politicians expressed public confidence in their authority to regulate rates, they seemed to harbor private doubts. A few months later, local politicians began lobbying the Illinois legislature for a law enabling all Illinois cities and towns to regulate gas rates. Peorians, along with Chicagoans, pushed hard for the statewide version of the Enabling Act in 1905.[41]

Peoria gas producers sued, claiming that the ordinance was confiscatory. The city did not challenge the claim that a 75-cent rate was unreasonably low. Instead, the city argued, producers were not entitled to any Fourteenth Amendment protection because they were in violation of Illinois law. Under Illinois's antitrust laws, if Peoria gas companies conspired to fix prices, their customers were under no legal obligation to pay for any gas they received while the conspiracy was in effect. This, Peoria authorities believed, allowed the city to set whatever rates it wanted. After all, if local gas companies conspired to fix rates, the law allowed consumers to receive gas for free. Producers were lucky to get 75 cents.[42]

The U.S. Supreme Court resolved the dispute in January 1906. The Court sympathized with the Peoria authorities on many counts. Producers probably violated Illinois' antitrust laws when they conspired to raise their prices to $1.15 in July 1900. The city probably could have required gas producers to charge 75 cents if producers had continued to violate the state's antitrust laws. The Court, however, observed that after January 1901, Peoria's two gas companies charged different rates. From this, the Court concluded that Peoria gas companies did not continue violating Illinois antitrust law. Because gas producers no longer violated Illinois's antitrust laws, they could not be denied Fourteenth Amendment protection. The Court refused to enforce the 75-cent rate ordinance.[43]

Summary

Chicago authorities used gas rates in local politics. Politics did not always work against gas companies, but it usually did. Electoral politics cut against the Peoples Gas Company in 1900 and in 1911. Partisan politics worked in favor of the company in 1906; however, even here the rate set by the city resulted in the largest reduction in gas rates seen in over two decades. Gas producers' immobile investments allowed local authorities to politicize gas rates. If capital had been mobile, the threat of exit would have undermined the political expediency of 70-cent gas. Arbitrary and onerous regulations would have driven gas producers out of the city. Presumably, such an exodus would have cost politicians many more votes than it won them.

Emphasizing the politicization of gas rates, it is easy to lose sight of an important point. Chicago gas companies were not innocent victims of local politics. On the contrary, local politics was a response to their efforts to monopolize the gas industry. Chicago politicians began regulating gas rates because of consumers' complaints that rates were too high. Consumers were right. After the gas acts, producers enjoyed and exploited substantial market power. There were only two other problems: low gas rates won votes and Chicago politicians pursued votes with as much deceit and greed as gas companies pursued profits.

A response to the relative price changes that followed the gas acts, the passage of the Enabling Act did not resolve the political battle over municipal regulation. The dubious constitutionality of the law meant that the city still did not have a clear and unambiguous claim to regulate rates. As a result, there remained pressure among both Chicago consumers and politicians for the city to secure more regulatory authority. Chicago gas companies, in contrast, wanted to prevent effective municipal regulation and the low rates that would prevail under such a regime. There were two ways for producers to deny the city ultimate regulatory control. Producers could challenge the constitutionality of the Enabling Act in the courts or they could secure passage of a law granting the state supreme regulatory control. Chicago gas companies favored the former, preferring as little regulatory interference as possible. However, they were willing to tolerate state regulation if that were the only way to prevent effective municipal regulation.

CHAPTER 7

State Regulation, 1914–24

In 1913, the Illinois legislature organized the Legislative Public Utilities Commission to assess the political demand for state utility regulation. The commission solicited volumes of testimony from utilities, consumers, municipal leaders, regulators from other states, and academics. According to the commission's report, consumers and politicians in Chicago opposed state regulation. They favored vesting the city council with supreme regulatory control. Limited evidence suggests that at least some voters in Springfield also favored local regulation. In smaller Illinois cities and towns, consumers generally preferred the creation of a state commission over home rule measures. Small towns may have wanted state regulation, rather than local regulation, because they wanted to commit to reasonable regulations and encourage the development of their gas markets. Unlike Chicago and Springfield, small towns often did not have gas service. This would be consistent with the voting analysis of the Enabling Act presented in the last chapter. Recall that small towns with little or no gas service opposed laws granting them regulatory power.[1]

When the general counsel for the Peoples Gas Light and Coke Company, James Meagher, testified before the legislative commission he said that he "opposed state regulation." This testimony contradicts Meagher's earlier position. As I explained in the last chapter, during the debate over the Enabling Act, Meagher had pleaded for the creation of a state utilities commission. The dubious constitutionality of the Enabling Act may explain Meagher's reversal in preference. If the general counsel believed that the courts would eventually declare the Enabling Act unconstitutional, he may have also believed that Peoples Gas would not need a state commission to forestall municipal regulation. Consistent with this view, Meagher testified in favor of a system of limited local control "with final recourse to the courts."[2]

Other utilities expressed mixed support for a state commission. The general counsel to Commonwealth Edison was "non-committal, but inclined to favor some system of [state] commission regulation." The president of the Chicago City Railway Company favored some form of limited municipal control but was willing to consider a state commission if its structure and power resembled Wisconsin's commission.[3]

In its final report, the legislative commission recommended the creation of a state utilities commission. The legislative commission's report recognized that a state regulatory body should protect the interests of both consumers and utilities. State regulation should prevent utilities from charging monopoly rates and, simultaneously, protect the utility against overzealous local regulators. The commission wrote (Illinois General Assembly 1913, 861):

> If municipalities are incapable of protecting their citizens for any reason from unjust exactions of public service corporations, it is the duty of the State to protect them in such a manner it deems right and proper. Conversely, if the citizens of any municipality, through their representatives, take such action as will destroy or confiscate public utility investments, it is likewise the duty of the State to assert its paramount authority to the end that justice may be accorded to citizens interested in such concerns.

According to the commission, Chicago's history illustrated the inadequacy of local regulation: "The Chicago City Council . . . demonstrated one of the weak points in the theory of exclusive local rule and regulation of utilities when they passed a 70-cent gas ordinance in response to local sentiment, against the recommendation of the city's own expert." The commission also lamented the unending litigation between Chicago gas companies and the city:

> The effort of the city of Chicago as well as many other cities of the State is to regulate rates and services of utility companies by law suit. . . . The method of thus supervising utilities is unscientific, expensive, vexatious and cumbersome. . . . In Chicago there has been almost constant litigation between the city and utilities, resulting in heavy burdens of taxation being placed upon its citizens and an extraordinary expense being incurred by utility companies.

State regulation, the commission went on to suggest, would prove a less costly way of resolving disputes. The commission foreshadowed Victor Goldberg's (1976) work.[4]

A Legislative History of the Public Utilities Act

The Illinois Public Utilities Act (IPUA) of 1913 grew out of house bill 907 (HB 907). In its original form, HB 907 provided that the governor would appoint a five-person commission—the Illinois Public Utilities Commission—to supervise Illinois utilities. The commission would control corporate franchises, the capitalization of utility companies, and the rates charged by utilities. The house passed the bill in this form on June 12, 1913, by a vote of 88 to 26. A few days after the vote, the *Tribune* reported that "the public service corporations now are for the house bill. Early in the session they were against any form of public utility legislation." The senate amended HB 907 and granted Chicago home rule. The home rule amendment gave the Chicago City Council exclusive regulatory control over Chicago utilities. If enacted, the home rule provision would have rendered moot questions about the Enabling Act's constitutionality. The senate also struck out the provisions giving the commission regulatory power over capitalization. In the end, however, the house refused to concur with the senate's amendments. On June 20, 1913, the legislature passed the bill in its original form.[5]

Chicago utilities opposed the senate's home rule amendment. The *Springfield Illinois State Register* reported: "it was quite significant during the fight that the corporation lobby vigorously opposed the 'home rule' feature, and was elated when that principle was finally eliminated." Similarly, the *Tribune* reported that "the big public utility corporations in Chicago" prefer a single state commission to a "double commission." The paper continued: "It is known that they do not want a separate commission in Chicago, which would be responsible originally to the present city government."[6]

Chicago politicians and consumers supported the home rule amendment. After the legislature passed the IPUA without it, the Chicago City Council adopted several resolutions protesting the measure. Council members denounced the IPUA as "vicious, infamous, and criminal." Alderman Charles Merriam called the act "the crowning triumph of corporation politics in Illinois." Now confronting a common foe, Mayor Carter Harrison found himself allied with his former mayoral opponent. Harrison argued: "The viciousness of this bill lies in the fact that home rule has been taken away from the city at the behest of the corporations. There is no disguising that fact. It is a corporation measure pure and simple." The city sent the governor the following telegram demanding that he veto the IPUA:

> We, the mayor and members of the city council of Chicago, urge you to veto the public utilities bill enacted by the recent general assembly. The city council in session tonight has unanimously adopted a protest against this bill and decided that the city council, civic organizations and citizens of Chicago wait upon you to present Chicago's protest.

Sixty-seven of the city's seventy aldermen signed the telegram. Mayor Harrison and fifty-nine aldermen followed up the telegram with a trip to Springfield where they personally demanded the governor's veto.[7]

Chicago business groups and citizens also protested. The Iroquois Club adopted a resolution calling the IPUA "the most iniquitous measure ever passed by the legislature of any state." The club also organized a delegation to meet with the governor. The Chicago Citizen's Association, the Hamilton Club, the Municipal Voter's League, the Woodlawn Business Men's Association, the Association of Commerce, and a group of twenty-four local liquor dealers took similar actions and asked the governor to veto the act. Citizens throughout the city organized spontaneous protests. For example, the *Tribune* reported that "[t]hree hundred [Chicago] residents gathered in a hall at Evanston and Wilson avenues and adopted resolutions calling on Gov. Dunne to veto the act and save Chicago's home rule privileges."[8]

Governor Edward Dunne was not impressed. Although he had initially threatened to veto the act if it did not contain a home rule provision for Chicago, the governor signed the IPUA into law on June 30, 1913. It was ironic. As Chicago's mayor in 1905, Dunne had pushed hard for the Enabling Act. As Illinois's governor in 1913, Dunne refused to veto a measure that effectively revoked the Enabling Act. In response to the complaints of Chicagoans, Dunne stated: "No criticism is offered to the bill except on the single point that it does not provide for home rule. Every other section has been approved by official representatives of Chicago."[9] Governors and mayors serve different constituencies.

The Effectiveness of State Utility Regulation

To assess the relative effectiveness of municipal and state regulation on gas prices, I compare Chicago gas prices with prices in other cities. I use the same cities here as in chapter 5 (see chap. 5 and app. B). Regulatory regimes in these cities remained constant for the period between 1878 and 1924. Chicago moved from municipal rate regulation to state regulation in 1914. Dividing gas prices in Chicago by the average price across the control group yields a ratio, that, over time, controls for industrywide changes in prices. Assuming that the 1900, 1905, and 1911 rate ordinances had been enforced, the ratio would have averaged 58 percent for the years of municipal regulation. During the period of state regulation, from 1914 through 1924, the ratio averaged 68 percent. In short, relative to gas prices in other U.S. cities, prices in Chicago were higher under state regulation than under municipal regulation.

An event study isolates the (anticipated) effects of state regulation on firm profitability. I calculate daily returns with data from the *Commercial and Financial Chronicle*.[10] The Dow Jones index serves to estimate the return on the market portfolio. Lagged and led market return terms are again included to control for the possibility of nonsynchronous trading. I employ the same estimating approach here as in the previous chapter. Cumulative excess returns are calculated using the parameter estimates from an out-of-sample model. Again, I regress CHI_t against MKT_t, MKT_{t-1}, and MKT_{t+1}. (The variables assume the same definitions as before.) This time, however, I use a sample of seventy-four observations, extending from March 2, 1913, through May 29.

Figure 6 plots the cumulative excess returns associated with passage of the IPUA. The market believed the move from municipal regulation to state regulation would have a small positive effect on firm profitability. With passage of the IPUA, the market value of the Peoples Gas Company increased by 5 percent.

Did Chicago Gas Companies Capture the State Utilities Commission?

The preceding data suggest that firm profitability and gas rates were higher under state regulation than municipal regulation. Does this mean that politicians and regulators at the state level ignored the interests of consumers? A close analysis of the mechanics of state regulation suggests not. At least for Chicago, the state utilities commission acted much like a court, searching for a middle ground between the demands of Peoples Gas and the city. When the commission strayed to one side or the other, it was not necessarily in favor of the gas company.

Consider the efforts of Peoples Gas to secure rate increases during the rapid inflation associated with World War I. In 1917, the company requested a 15 percent rate increase. The commission denied it. In January 1918, the company requested a 22 percent increase. Again the commission refused the increase. The company's contractual obligations with the city of Chicago prevented the commission from granting any rate changes before August 1918. In April 1918, the company modified its earlier request and asked for a 30 percent increase. Testifying before the utilities commission, the chairman of Peoples Gas, Samuel Insull, claimed that without a rate increase the company might have to declare bankruptcy. The stock market corroborated Insull's claim of financial distress. Between January 1917 and January 1918, the market value of the Peoples Gas Light and Coke Company fell nearly 50 percent. Figure 7 plots month-ending stock prices from 1897 through 1922. From figure 7, the drop in market value had no historical precedent. It also cannot be attrib-

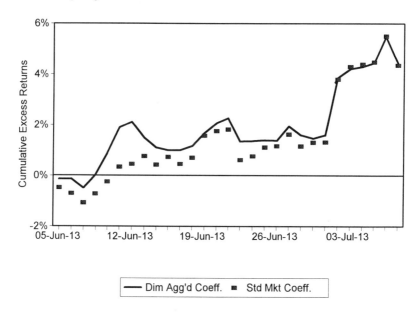

Fig. 6. Excess returns associated with passage of the public utilities act

uted to marketwide shocks because the market index did not crash. Less reliable accounting data reveal the same pattern. For the years 1917 and 1918, the company's income statements report losses.[11]

In July 1918, the utilities commission allowed Peoples Gas to increase its rates from 70 to 88 cents. Chicago authorities, however, demanded that the commission reopen the rate case. The city maintained that rates should be returned to 70 cents. At a re-hearing scheduled in April 1919, the commission reduced the company's rate to 85 cents. Rates remained at 85 cents until June 1920, when they were raised to $1.15. In August 1920, Peoples Gas requested permission to raise rates to $1.40. The company argued that the rate would allow it to earn an 8 percent return on its capital, which the company valued at $114 million. Chicago authorities responded by filing a petition with the commission. The city argued that the commission should lower rates, not raise them. The city maintained that the company should be allowed only a 7 percent return on capital. It also valued the company's capital at $55 million, less than 50 percent of the company's valuation. According to the city, the numbers entitled Peoples Gas to charge only $1. After a lengthy investigation, the commission ordered Peoples Gas to reduce its rates to $1.

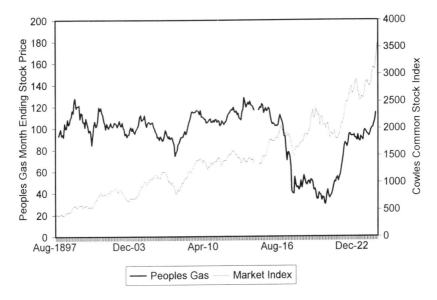

Fig. 7. Peoples Gas Light and Coke Co., month ending stock prices, 1897–1924 (the break in trading is due to World War I). (Data for stock prices of the Peoples Gas Light and Coke Company, from various issues of the *New York Times*, *Chicago Tribune*, and *Commercial and Financial Chronicle*. For the market index, see Cowles [1939].)

Explaining the Effectiveness of State and Municipal Regulation

Although not pawns to utilities, state regulators sympathized more with producers' interests than did municipal regulators. The framework constructed in chapter 2 suggests three reasons gas consumers, through their power at the ballot box, would have monitored local regulators better than state regulators. First, under municipal regulation, the city council regulated gas rates directly. Under state regulation, the state legislature regulated rates indirectly, through a commission. The commission introduced an additional layer of monitoring costs for voters. Voters monitored the state legislators, who then monitored the utility commissioners. Alderman Charles Merriam expressed a similar argument: "The real reason why many corporations prefer state to local control is not that one is more 'political' than the other, but that the indirect pressure of the state electorate is preferred to the direct pressure of the local electorate."[12]

Second, local legislators represented smaller, more geographically concentrated constituencies than state legislators. As a result, the free-rider problems that typically confound effective voter monitoring would have been less severe under municipal regulation than under state regulation.

Third, utility rates were a salient issue in local politics. In Chicago, gas rates were front-page news. As Carter Harrison's 1911 campaign illustrates, local politicians faced strong electoral incentives to promise and deliver low utility rates. Utility rates assumed less importance at the state level because state legislators dealt with more issues than local legislators. There were many other issues state politicians could use to win votes.

The Stability of State Regulation

Unlike earlier regulatory regimes, state regulation endured. Twice, Chicago politicians lobbied the legislature to attach a home rule amendment to the IPUA of 1913. In 1917, a special house committee recommended a home rule bill for Chicago. Several forces conspired against the bill. Chicago gas and electric companies opposed the measure, as did legislators from regions outside Chicago. In smaller municipalities, consumers and local politicians thought that state regulation worked well. Beyond this, Chicago consumers themselves seemed to lack the political will necessary to push the bill through. A local referendum ballot taken on April 7, 1914, posed the following question to Chicago voters: "Shall the State Legislature amend the act creating a State Public Utilities Commission, approved June 30, 1913, so as to provide for home rule and control by the city of Chicago of public utilities within the city?" The result: 182,335 Chicagoans favored such an amendment; 173,335 opposed it.[13] Compare this vote with the referendum vote on the Enabling Act: as noted in chapter 6, nearly 125,000 Chicagoans voted in favor of the Enabling Act, and only 20,504 voted against it.

In 1921, amid claims that the state commission had been captured by utilities, supporters of home rule tried again to amend the IPUA. Home rule proponents introduced a bill that contained two provisions. The first provision abolished the Illinois Public Utilities Commission and created the Illinois Commerce Commission. The new commission had the same powers as its predecessor but a slightly different administrative structure. The second provision granted all Illinois municipalities the power to regulate utility rates, subject to a local referendum vote. If voters in a given locality opposed municipal control, the state commission would retain regulatory control. The bill passed but not before Illinois utilities emasculated the municipal regulation provision. A state commission continued to regulate Illinois utilities.[14]

What explains the stability of state regulation? Everyone in Chicago—

consumers, local politicians, and producers—saw state regulation as a second-best regulatory outcome. Chicago gas companies tolerated state regulation only because they saw it as a politically expedient way to undermine the regulatory authority of the Chicago City Council. In a perfect world, they would not have been subject to any regulatory oversight, by either state or local authorities. As Roger Sullivan, president of the Ogden Gas Company, so eloquently phrased it: "We . . . don't want any legislation," but "if we have to lose something we'd rather it should be a little toe [state regulation by commission] than a big one [municipal regulation by the city council]."[15] Similarly, consumers and local politicians came to prefer state regulation over no regulation because the former put at least some limits on producers' monopoly power. In a perfect world, consumers and local politicians would have had the city council, not a state commission, regulate gas rates. In short, gas companies preferred no regulation to state regulation and state regulation over municipal regulation, while consumers and local politicians preferred municipal regulation to state regulation and state regulation over no regulation.

Compare the incentives consumers and producers had to alter the IPUA with their incentives to alter earlier legislation like the gas acts and the Enabling Act. The marginal benefits to consumers of moving from state regulation to municipal regulation were less than those of moving from a world without any regulation to a world with municipal regulation. Consumers faced stronger incentives to overturn the gas acts than they did to overturn the IPUA. Conversely, the marginal benefits to gas producers of moving from a world with state regulation to a world with no regulation were less than those of moving from a world with municipal regulation to a world with no rate regulation. Producers faced stronger incentives to overturn the Enabling Act than they did to overturn state regulation.

Formal Studies of State Utility Regulation

The effectiveness of state utility regulation is a contentious question. In a seminal paper, Stigler and Friedland (1962) set up a natural experiment. They analyze the prices and profits of electricity utilities during the early twentieth century. During that period, regulatory regimes varied across states. Some states had utility commissions; some did not. Stigler and Friedland find that rates and profits were not significantly lower in states with utility commissions. From this, they conclude that state regulation allowed utility companies to charge high rates and earn monopoly profits. In drawing this conclusion, Stigler and Friedland assume that in states without regulatory commissions, utilities operated without any regulatory constraints and were, therefore, able to charge monopoly rates and earn monopoly profits. As Priest (1993) suggests, it is a problematic assumption. Even in states without regulatory commissions, municipal regulations put limits on the behavior of utility companies. Sometimes local authorities directly regulated rates, as they did in Chicago after the Enabling Act. Other times, local authorities used franchise contracts and competition.

Moore (1970) and Meyer and Leland (1980) estimate demand and cost equations to isolate the effects of regulation. Moore uses a cross section of electric utilities operating in 1962. He finds that state regulation lowered rates from monopoly levels by only 3 percent. Meyer and Leland pool data from forty-eight states over the period 1969 through 1974. These data, and the estimating procedure, allow for the possibility that the effectiveness of regulation varies over time and across space. Allowing for this possibility distinguishes Meyer and Leland's study from earlier work. They find "pervasive irregularity in regulatory impact across states and widespread and substantial benefits being conferred by rate of return regulation" (Meyer and Leland 1980, 562).

Jarrell (1978) isolates the political demand for state utility regulation. Suppose consumers demanded regulation to protect them against monopoly rates. If so, one would expect states where utilities charged the highest rates and earned the most profits to have been the first to create utility commissions. Alternatively, suppose utilities demanded regulation to protect them against the low rates set by municipal regulators. In that case, one would expect states where utilities charged the lowest rates and earned the lowest profits to have been the first to create utility commissions. Jarrell divides states into two groups, early regulated states and later regulated states. Early regulated states created utility commissions between 1912 and 1917; later regulated states created utility commissions after 1917. After adjusting for cross-state variations in demand and cost conditions, Jarrell finds that electric utilities in early regulated states charged lower rates and earned lower profits than utilities in later regulated states.

Jarrell concludes that municipal authorities set competitive rates that allowed producers a reasonable return while state regulators set rates close to monopoly levels. He rejects the idea that municipal authorities promoted unreasonably low rates. He rejects this idea after calculating the ratio of average revenue to average cost for each state. For both early regulated states and later regulated states the mean ratio exceeded one. On average, electric utilities covered their costs.

Jarrell's central finding—that utilities lobbied for state regulation to undermine the hostile policies of local authorities—is unassailable. His ancillary claim—that municipal authorities promoted reasonable and competitive rates—is less convincing. There are three problems. First, comparing costs and revenues says little about the rates set by local authorities. It only offers indirect evidence on the rates allowed by the courts. In Chicago, for example, gas companies twice used the courts to block rates they claimed were confiscatory. Second, in calculating his revenue-to-cost ratios, Jarrell combines states that allowed municipal rate regulation with states that prohibited municipal rate regulation. As in Illinois, some state constitutions prohibited municipal governments from regulating rates without special enabling legislation. Other states, however, empowered municipal governments to regulate rates.[16] Third, Jarrell's revenue-to-cost ratios are averages. They only speak to the performance of the mean firm. Little is known about the distribution of firms that fell below the mean. This is unfortunate because the firms below the mean were the firms most affected by municipal regulation. It seems plausible that it was these below-the-mean firms, those hardest hit by municipal regulation, that pushed the hardest for state regulation.

Comparisons

In Illinois, the battle over state regulation centered on the issue of home rule. Local politicians wanted it. Utilities did not. The battle over state regulation followed a similar pattern in Ohio. Ohio utilities opposed state regulation bills until the state legislature removed their home rule provisions. In 1911, the Ohio legislature passed its own public utilities act. The law gave a state commission ultimate regulatory control. In Chicago, gas companies tolerated state regulation because they saw the alternative, municipal control, as arbitrary and politicized. Similarly, in California utilities lobbied for state regulation, in part, to forestall municipal control. The vice president of the Pacific Gas and Electric Company argued that under municipal regulation, corporations were "at the mercy of as pitiless a pack of howling destroyers, as would the lonely traveller on the Siberian steppes be against the gaunt and hungry wolves." The company vice president advocated state regulation, in part, because state commissions would set rates in "calm deliberation and not in political heat." Officials from the Los Angeles Gas and Electric Company also demanded state regulation "on account of the growing desire on the part of our city governments to regulate our affairs."[17]

Summary

In 1913, Illinois authorities confronted a dilemma. Left unchecked, Chicago gas companies charged monopoly rates. The Chicago City Council had the authority to keep gas rates in check. Unfortunately, it abused that authority. Illinois legislators resolved the dilemma by creating a state utilities commission. Legislators hoped that the commission would balance the interests of both consumers and companies. The commission would protect consumers against monopoly rates; the commission would protect gas companies against the arbitrary and politicized policies of the Chicago City Council. While other solutions may have worked better, state regulation worked reasonably well. The state commission set rates higher than local authorities, but at the same time it did not run roughshod over the interests of consumers. Finally, unlike earlier regulatory devices, state regulation persisted. It did not persist because everybody loved it. It persisted because the relative price changes it generated were not large enough to make it profitable for either consumers or producers to secure further regulatory change.

CHAPTER 8

Conclusions

As in Chicago, water gas wrought entry and competition to gas markets in Atlanta, Baltimore, Buffalo, Cleveland, and New York. As in Chicago, consolidation and merger eventually thwarted competition in these cities. As in Chicago, gas companies sometimes used politics and regulation to prevent entry and competition. In Cincinnati and Cleveland, gas companies bribed local authorities to stop entry; in New Jersey, gas companies enjoyed the protection of the gas act, a special incorporation law; and elsewhere frontage laws limited entry. As in Chicago, city authorities responded to producers' efforts to monopolize local gas markets. In Detroit, they revoked the franchise of a gas company that colluded; in Peoria, they passed an ordinance requiring a large rate reduction. As in Chicago, city councils often went too far in taming local monopolies. In Cleveland, Memphis, and Peoria, local authorities set rates without any investigation into the costs of manufacturing and distributing gas; in California and Wisconsin, utilities claimed that local authorities used the promise of low rates to win votes. As in Chicago, gas companies in California and Ohio came to see state regulation as a politically expedient way to undermine local regulators. As my comments in the "Comparisons" section of chapters 3 through 7 show, these parallels share a common theme: the forces at work in Chicago were also at work in other cities.

Chicago's experience suggests four lessons. First, by itself, producer support for a particular economic policy does not necessarily imply that the policy is inefficient or even against something one might call the public interest. Chicago gas companies supported state regulation only because municipal control was arbitrary and politicized—Chicago regulators used low gas rates to promote electoral support, not economic efficiency. In this context, the fact that utilities lobbied for and supported state regulation does not have the same negative efficiency implications as it otherwise might. In discussing the origins of railroad regulation, Hovenkamp develops the same idea. He writes (Hovenkamp 1991, 136):

Various interests petition legislative bodies for regulation that closes their market to new entry or guarantees their profit margins. A sound regulatory policy must distinguish these self-serving requests for protection from competition from those occasions when bona-fide market failures make regulation necessary. The mere fact that the proposed regulation benefits the regulated firm does not divide the territory. Often the burden of market failure falls on the firms themselves. In such cases the firms may clamor for regulation *and* regulation may serve the public interests as well.

Second, a little historical knowledge is a dangerous thing. By selectively reading Chicago's history, I could find evidence to support any of the prevailing interpretations of utility regulation. By pointing to the many antitrust suits against Chicago gas producers and their unending attempts to combine, I could make a fair case for the natural monopoly interpretation. By pointing to producers' lobbying efforts and the fact that gas rates were higher under state regulation than under municipal regulation, I could make a strong case for the Chicago school interpretation. By pointing to producers' huge investment in gas mains and the capriciousness of Chicago politicians, I could make an even stronger case for the relational contracting interpretation. The key to pulling together these otherwise divergent views lies in considering the larger historical experience.

Third, state utility commissions did not just suddenly appear when consumers discovered unregulated natural monopolies did not charge low prices or, alternatively, when utilities discovered that they could earn more money if they were regulated. Utility commissions evolved out of a larger process of historical change. Deliberate, human action animated change; consumers and local politicians lobbied for antitrust regulation and the Enabling Act; producers lobbied for the gas acts and state regulation. Technology determined the nature of change. That is, the unique technological structure of the gas industry dictated that change be legal and political. The geographic specificity of gas mains prevented local gas companies from exiting the Chicago area. Because producers could not exit, they were forced to resolve their differences with the city through the courts and the state legislature. This insight helps explain the unique regulatory experience of gas companies and other utilities.

Fourth, as the relational contracting interpretation suggests, state regulation emulated the contractual institutions of the nineteenth century. During the nineteenth century, market forces, although they did not work perfectly, limited producers' ability to charge monopoly rates and provide poor service. The Illinois Constitution prohibited municipal rate regulation, which helped prevent local politicians from using the threat of unreasonably low rates to blackmail utilities or win votes from consumers. Passage of the gas acts and the Enabling Act undermined these institutions.

Erecting a prohibitive entry barrier and removing the legal obstacles to merger, the gas acts helped producers suppress market forces. Removing the constitutional prohibition against municipal rate regulation, the Enabling Act made it easier for Chicago politicians to use gas rates as a political device. Passage of the Illinois Public Utilities Act (IPUA) rehabilitated the market mechanism and the state constitution. As market forces had before the gas acts, state regulation kept producers' monopoly power in check. As the state constitution had done before the Enabling Act, state regulation prevented local politicians from using gas rates as a political device.

Part 3: Appendixes

Appendix A

Manufacturing Coal and Water Gas

Producers manufactured coal gas by filling a series of fire clay boxes, called retorts, with several tons of coal. Each retort measured fourteen to twenty inches in diameter and eighteen to twenty feet in length. For gas works as large those in Chicago, the retort house—the container that held all the retorts—measured about eighty feet in length, fifty-five feet in width, and contained about sixteen separate retorts. Once workers filled the retorts with coal, they distilled a gas by heating the coal to a temperature of 1,000 to 2,500 degrees Fahrenheit for five to sixty hours (Richards 1877, 93, 99–105).

In its primary form, the gas produced in the retorts contained ammonia, sulfur, and tar. Manufacturers removed each of these impurities, at least partially, before distributing the gas to consumers. Manufacturers removed the ammonia because it damaged gas meters and fixtures. Manufacturers removed the sulfur because it had an unpleasant smell and because it left a dirty residue on furniture and clothing. Manufacturers removed the tar because it built up in mains and in consumers' lighting fixtures. Also, gas producers often sold the ammonia and tar residuals for other industrial uses (Richards 1877, 108, 126, 135–40, 146).

Once distilled, the coal gas was forced out of the retort into a condenser. The condenser removed virtually all the tar, a small amount of ammonia, and some other impurities. In the condenser, the gas flowed over a few inches of water. As the gas contacted the water, it cooled. Cooling the gas caused elements of tar and ammonia to condense. The condensed tar and ammonia fell into the water below and were then drained away. Made of cast iron, condensers stood eighteen-feet high with several rows of condensing pipes. Condensing pipes measured up to three feet in diameter (Richards 1877, 108–17).

After the condenser removed the tar, a washer or scrubber removed the residual ammonia. In washing gas, manufacturers forced the gas through a few inches of water and then through a flat metal plate called a dashboard. The dashboard had rows of circular holes not more than one-quarter inch in diameter. As the gas passed through the dashboard, it separated and lost elements of ammonia. During the late nineteenth century, manufacturers abandoned the technique of washing the gas in favor of a scrubber process; washing the gas not only removed the ammonia, it also removed some of the illuminating power of the gas. In scrubbing gas, manufacturers removed the ammonia by spraying the gas with water as it passed through a bed of coke (Richards 1877, 126–34).

The purifier removed elements of sulfur from the gas, the final stage of the manufacturing process. The purifier was a large, typically iron, vessel that contained numerous shelves. The shelves were perforated so that the coal gas could pass through them. On top of the shelves, workers placed a layer of damp lime. Forcing the gas through the shelves of lime removed the sulfur. After it left the purifier, the gas was stored in large cast-iron or brick holders before being distributed. Gas holders stood fifteen feet tall and measured forty-five feet around (Richards 1877, 135–57, 163–90).

Water gas became commercially viable during the 1870s. In making water gas, producers passed steam and a vaporized oil through the incandescent beds of coal to increase the lighting power of the gas. Figure 8 depicts a Lowe water gas apparatus, an early, but frequently used water gas technology. The manufacturing process began in the generator, (section A in fig. 8). The generator was lined with firebrick and filled with anthracite coal or coke. Air blasts from beneath the generator chamber fired the coal (or coke) and distilled a gas. This gas was then forced through section C to section B, known as a superheater; firebricks filled the superheater. Once the gas reached the superheater, a second air blast burned the gas and heated the firebricks. After the bricks in the superheater reached the proper temperature, the air blasts ceased and steam was admitted beneath the coals in the generator (section A). Passing the steam through the incandescent bed of coal created a nonluminous water gas which was mixed with oil vapors introduced at the top of the generator. Then the oil and steam gases went through section C to the superheater. In the superheater, the gases contacted the heated firebricks and were fixed—they were combined into a single, permanent illuminating gas. Finally, washers and scrubbers purified the gas just as in the production of ordinary coal gas (Shelton 1889).

Appendix B

Measuring the Effects of Market Entry, Antitrust Regulation, and the Gas Acts

As figure 9 illustrates, nominal gas prices in Chicago fell steadily from $1.25 to $1 between 1888 and 1897. Was this gradual reduction in price the result of an increasingly competitive gas market? Or, alternatively, was it the result of some other shock, such as an industrywide reduction in input prices or an economywide decline in the general price level? To control for industrywide (as well as economywide) shocks, I compare gas prices in Chicago with prices in the following eight cities: Wilmington, Delaware; Burlington, Iowa; Iowa City, Iowa; Sioux City, Iowa; Danville, Kentucky; Owensboro, Kentucky; Shelbyville, Kentucky; and Minneapolis, Minnesota. These cities act as a control group. They were similar to Chicago except that their gas markets were not subject to antitrust regulation and experienced no market entry over this period.

Figure 10 plots the ratio of gas prices in Chicago to the average price of gas in the control group cities. Ratio-West equals the price of gas on Chicago's west side divided by the average control group price; Ratio-No., So. equals the price of gas on Chicago's north and south sides divided by the average control group price. Note that gas prices in Chicago averaged only 60 percent of gas prices in the control group cities. Coal, oil, and other inputs were cheaper in Chicago than in these other cities (see Chicago City Council 1906, 43–50, and the *Brown's Directory of American Gas Companies,* volumes 1916–22). As figure 10 shows, prices in Chicago behaved only modestly better than gas prices in markets that were not subject to new market entry or antitrust regulation. Note, however, that this ratio should be interpreted cautiously. If some unidentified variable influenced gas prices in Chicago but not in the control group cities, or vice versa, the ratio could be misleading.

Figure 9 shows that nominal gas prices in Chicago fell steadily until 1897, the year the gas acts were passed. Gas rates then remained constant until 1905, the year the city acquired the authority to regulate rates. Certainly factors other than the passage of the gas acts could have caused

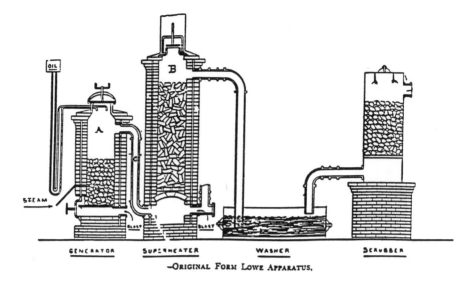

Fig. 8. Lowe water gas apparatus, circa 1873. (Source: Shelton [1889].)

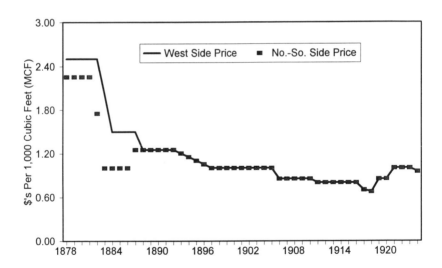

Fig. 9. Nominal gas rates in Chicago, 1878–1924. (Data from the same source as figure 3.)

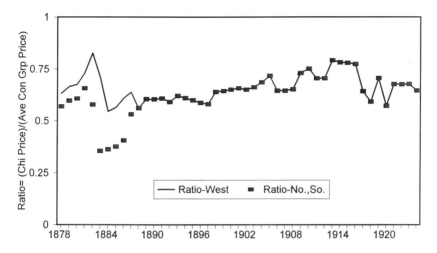

Fig. 10. Chicago gas prices as a percentage of gas prices in control group cities. (Data for Chicago gas prices are the same as for figure 3. For prices in other cities, see *Brown's Directory of American Gas Companies,* volumes 1887–1924. The 1887 volume contains a history of prices back to 1873.)

Chicago gas prices to stop falling. To control for at least some of these other factors, I again compare gas prices in Chicago to gas prices in the cities identified earlier. Figure 10 shows that the ratio of prices in Chicago to prices in the control group began to rise after 1897; prices in cities that did not have laws like the gas acts continued to fall after 1897. As explained in chapter 5, this is consistent with the hypothesis that the gas acts caused prices in Chicago to have been higher than they otherwise would have been.

One way to measure how market entry, antitrust enforcement, and the gas acts affected firm profitability would be to look at producers' income statements. Although the simplicity of such an analysis is attractive, considering accounting data in isolation of other evidence can be misleading. Because income statements are published yearly, it is often impossible to separate the effects of a new market entrant (or a court-ordered reorganization) from other shocks that occurred during the same year (e.g., a dramatic change in the price of a key input).

One way to solve this problem is by examining stock prices. For example, if investors in Chicago gas securities generally believed that a new entrant would reduce the profitability of incumbent firms, the stock price of Chicago gas companies would have fallen when investors learned that a new firm was about to enter. Alternatively, if investors believed that a new entrant would not reduce profitability, stock prices would have remained constant when investors learned of the new firm. Because the behavior of stock prices can be examined over a relatively small event window it is easier to separate the effects of entry from other potentially confounding events. Also, it is a straightforward process to separate changes in stock prices that result from marketwide shocks from those changes that result from shocks unique to the firm under consideration.

Event study methodology offers a simple way of isolating how the stock price of a firm reacts to changes in its operating environment. The event study approach employed here assumes that the predicted or normal rate of return for any security i over period t, $PRET_{it}$, can be expressed as,

$$PRET_{it} = a + b\ MKT_t, \tag{1}$$

where MKT_t is the realized rate of return on the market portfolio during period t. The difference between the realized or actual rate of return (RET_{it}) and the normal rate of return ($PRET_{it}$) during period t, e_{it}, is defined as an excess return,

$$e_{it} = RET_{it} - PRET_{it}. \tag{2}$$

It is hypothesized that the occurrence of extraordinary events that affect only security i should induce excess returns that are large and significantly different from zero. In this context, the actual value of e_{it} during an event period has economic meaning: it provides a measure of how much the market value of the firm has changed as a result of the event. The residual e_{it} reflects investors' best guesses about the financial effects of the event. These are well-informed guesses; the firm's investors (owners) have a strong economic incentive to understand the financial consequences of changes in their firm's operating environment (see Fama et al. 1969 for a general discussion of event study methodology; see Binder 1985 and 1988 for a discussion of the use of event studies to analyze the effects of regulation).

I use weekly data to estimate the parameters described in equation (1). I calculate the weekly returns of the Chicago Gas (Trust) Company with data from the *Commercial and Financial Chronicle* and the *New York Times*. The data begin with the week ending September 21, 1889, and end with the week ending September 27, 1897. Dividend rates and dates of payment for the gas company are identified with the *Commercial and Financial Chronicle*. I use the Dow index to calculate the returns on the market portfolio.

Table 7 identifies the events that I hypothesize affected the market value of the Chicago Gas (Trust) Company. The dates associated with each event are arrived at by using accounts found in the popular and financial press. One common objection to event studies is that the exact date the market acquires new information about an event is often shrouded in uncertainty. This uncertainty reduces the power of event studies and may

TABLE 7. Description of Key Events

Date[a]	Event Name	Event Description[b]
05/27/89	LOWCRT	Lower court upheld legality of holding company. (+)
12/02/89	SUPCRT1	Illinois Supreme Court broke up holding company. (−)
03/03/90	CHARFILE	F. M. Charlton filed suit against holding company. (−)
03/24/90	NOREHEAR	Illinois Supreme Court declined to re-hear case against holding company. (−)
04/07/90	CHARMOT	Charlton withdrew one of his actions against the holding company. (+)
05/02/90	CHARREC	Judge appointed receiver in Charlton suit. (−)
05/30/90	CHARDIS	Charlton suit was dismissed. (+)
09/22/90	DENY	Court denied holding company's motion. (−)
10/03/90	PROCED	Court ruled in favor of holding company. (+)
11/10/90	SUPCRT2	Illinois Supreme Court issued order prohibiting the holding company from owning any stock. (−)
12/22/90	ECON1	Economic Gas Company received fuel gas ordinance. (−)
01/26/91	REORG1	Holding company announced reorganization. (+)
04/13/91	REORG2	Holding company announced reorganization plan. (+)
06/29/91	ECON2	Council introduced Economic lighting ordinance. (−)
07/13/91	ECON3	Council overrode mayor's veto of ordinance. (−)
02/23/92	ECON4	Gas trust acquired Economic. (+)
03/28/92	MUTUAL	Mutual Company began selling fuel gas. (−)
04/30/94	SUIT	Attorney general brought suit against gas trust. (−)
07/02/94	SUITOVER	Suit resolved on terms favorable to gas trust. (+)
07/16/94	UNIVERS1	City council passed Universal franchise ordinance. (−)
07/23/94	UNIVERS2	Council overrode mayor's veto of franchise. (−)
10/08/94	UNIVERS3	Gas trust and Universal colluded. (−)
02/25/95	OGDEN1	City council passed Ogden franchise ordinance. (−)
03/04/95	OGDEN2	Mayor approved Ogden franchise. (−)
07/01/95	GACTS1	Legislature failed to override governor's veto of the frontage act. (−)
09/23/95	PAPERS1	Gas trust submitted articles of consolidation. (+)
10/07/95	PAPERS2	Gas trust announced exact reorganization plan. (+)
02/10/96	PAPERS3	Attorney general rejected reorganization plan. (−)
02/24/96	PAPERS4	Secretary of state refused articles of consolidation. (−)
05/24/97	GACTS2	Legislature failed to pass frontage and consolidation bills. (−)
06/07/97	GACTS3	Legislature reconsidered and passed frontage and consolidation bills. (+)

[a]Week ending date of event.

[b](+) indicates that the event is expected to have had a positive effect on the firm's value; (−) indicates that the event is expected to have had a negative effect on market value.

seriously understate the perceived financial effects of an event (Brown and Warner 1985). For example, although the Chicago City Council passed the ordinance allowing the Universal Gas Company to begin operations on July 16, 1894, the press indicated that such an ordinance would be passed several weeks earlier. Similarly, the market appears to have anticipated some of the antitrust rulings against the Chicago Gas Company (see *Chicago Tribune,* July 18, 1894, 1–2, and June 29, 1894, 4).

Gilligan and Krehbiel (1988) address this problem by examining several different event windows. In the estimation here, I consider two alternative event windows, a one-week event window and a four-week event window. For the one-week event window, I code event dummies so that for each event they equal 1 only during the event week identified in table 7. For the four-week event window, I code event dummies so that they equal 1 for the two weeks preceding, the week of, and the week following the event week as identified in table 7.

In the final estimation, the events identified in table 7 are grouped and then used as explanatory variables in an estimation of the market model. For example, grouping together all of the events associated with the entry of new firms creates the dummy variable *ENTRY; ENTRY* assumes a value of 1 for the weeks that the Ogden, Universal, and Economic received franchises. The coefficient on *ENTRY* measures the average effect of new market entrants on the value of the gas trust. Similarly, grouping all of the events associated with the producers' efforts to reorganize in response to the state's antitrust suits creates the dummy variable *REORG; REORG* assumes a value of 1 for the week that the holding company reorganized as a trust, the week that the trust announced a second reorganization plan, and so on. The identical approach is used to construct the variables *COURT,* which measures the average effect of the state's antitrust suits; *GASACTS,* which measures the average effect of the events associated with passage of the gas acts; and *COLLUDE,* which measures the average effect of the events associated with producers' attempts to combine with their new entrants. Table 8 summarizes the exact definitions of these variables.

With these groupings, I regress CHI_t against MKT_t, *COURT, REORG, ENTRY, COLLUDE* and *GASACTS. CHI_t* is the realized rate of return for the Chicago Gas (Trust) Company during week t. MKT_t is the realized rate of return on the market portfolio for week t. *COURT, REORG, ENTRY, COLLUDE,* and *GASACTS* are described earlier in the text and defined in table 8. In the regression, I also interact year dummies with the intercept and market return terms. The year dummies control for structural shifts in the relationship between the market and the gas trust.

Table 9 reports the regression results. Similar to Gilligan and Krehbiel (1988), the results are not always robust to changes in the event window. When a one-week event window is used, only *COURT* and *GASACTS* are significant. On average, each antitrust decision induced negative excess returns of 5 or 6 percent. Events associated with the passage of the gas acts induced excess returns of 3 percent. When a four-week

TABLE 8. Event Group Variables

Variable Definition*
COURT = (–1)∗LOWCRT + SUPCRT1 + CHARFILE + NOHEAR + (–1)∗CHARMOT + CHARREC + (–1)∗CHARDIS + DENY + (–1)∗PROCED + SUPCRT2 + SUIT + (–1)∗SUITOVER + PAPERS3 + PAPERS4
REORG = REORG1 + REORG2 + PAPERS1 + PAPERS2
ENTRY = ECON1 + ECON2 + ECON3 + MUTUAL + UNIVERS1 + UNIVERS2 + OGDEN1 + OGDEN2
COLLUDE = ECON4 + UNIVERS3
GASACTS = (–1)∗GACTS1 + (–1)∗GACTS2 + GACTS3

Note: Some event dummies are multiplied by negative one (–1) so all events in the group have the same predicted sign. The predicted signs follow: *COURT* (–); *REORG* (+); *ENTRY* (–); *COLLUDE* (+); and *GASACTS* (+).

TABLE 9. Event Study Results

Selected Variables	One Week Event Window		Four Week Event Window	
COURT (–)	–0.057	(5.222)***	–0.020	(3.477)***
REORG (+)	–0.018	(0.875)	0.020	(2.042)**
ENTRY (–)	–0.012	(0.143)*	–0.010	(1.665)*
COLLUDE (+)	0.019	(0.654)	–0.001	(0.015)
GASACTS (+)	0.034	(1.447)*	0.023	(1.562)*
MKT	0.718	(3.561)***	0.774	(3.837)***
INTERCEPT	0.004	(0.733)	0.004	(0.717)
Number of observations	453		453	
Adj. R^2	.	0.431		0.419
Mean of dependent variable (CHI)	0.004		0.004	

Notes: Variables not reported include the following: the individual year dummies, which control for shifts in the intercept from year to year, and year dummies interacted with the market return, *MKT,* which control for shifts in the relationship between the *MKT* and Chicago returns. *t*-statistics are reported in parentheses.
*Significant at 0.10 percent.
**Significant at 0.05 percent.
***Significant at 0.01 percent.

event window is used, *ENTRY* and *REORG,* as well as *COURT* and *GAS-ACTS,* are significant. The significance of *REORG* in this estimation provides weak evidence that producers were able to recoup some of the losses induced by the state's antitrust actions. The significance of *ENTRY* offers similarly weak evidence on the efficacy of new market entry.

Notes

Chapter 1

1. For state regulation during the nineteenth century, see Stotz and Jamison 1938, 446–49. For a complete survey of the regulatory powers of municipalities in different states, see Von Sinderen 1906. Pond (1906) provides a detailed analysis of the legal restrictions on municipal corporations. See also the following cases: *Norwich Gas Light Company v. The Norwich City Gas Company*, 25 Conn. 19 (1856); *City of LaHarpe v. Elm Township Gas, Light, Fuel & Power Company*, 69 Kan. 97 (1904); *Kentucky Heating Company v. Louisville Gas Company*, 23 Ky. Law Rep. 730 (1901); *Citizens' Gaslight Company v. Louisville Gas Company*, 81 Ky. 263 (1883); *City of Noblesville v. Noblesville Gas & Improvement Company*, 157 Ind. 162 (1901); *Mills v. City of Chicago, et al.*, 127 Fed. 731 (1904); and *Worcester Gaslight Company v. City of Worcester*, 110 Mass. 353 (1872). For the creation of state utility commissions, see Stigler and Friedland 1962 and Stotz and Jamison 1938, 450.

2. See, for example, Stotz and Jamison 1938, 421–22.

3. Quotations from Demsetz 1968, 59, 68. See also Jarrell 1978.

4. See Goldberg 1976 and Williamson 1985, 327–64, for general statements of the relational contracting approach.

5. The city might grant another company the right to use the streets but then it would have to again incur the costs of entry: namely, streets in disrepair, the risk that the streets would not be returned to their former condition once the company finished installing its mains, and so on. See, generally, Jacobson 1989.

6. To date, Priest 1993 offers the most developed expression of the relational contracting explanation as it applies to the origins of utility regulation. Summarizing Priest's basic argument, Miller 1993, 325, writes: "As Priest paints the picture, early public utility regulation closely resembled long-term relational contracting. The city council and the utility were both buyers and sellers of the others' assets or services. Thus regulation took the form of negotiation and renegotiation of long-term contracts of the sort that has become familiar in the analysis of many private contractual settings. The [state] commission form of regulation, which replaced municipal-franchise-type regulation in the early 1900s, is then seen as not representing any sort of fundamental shift in the regulation of public utilities."

7. Priest 1993 discusses the implications of the Chicago school interpretation of utility regulation. Hovenkamp 1991, 132–37, compares the Chicago school inter-

pretation of regulation more generally to the work of Gabriel Kolko and other historians sympathetic to the capture hypothesis.

8. See Blackford 1970; McDonald 1957, 117–19; McDonald 1958; and Thelen 1972, 286–87.

9. See the preceding discussion and citations.

10. The new institutional economics highlights the importance of institutions and institutional change in many different contexts. For example, Williamson 1985 explores the importance of institutions in the face of asset-specific investment. (The relational contracting literature is a subset of the new institutional economics.) North 1981 and 1990 explores how institutions and institutional change affect economic growth and, in turn, are affected by growth. Shepsle and Weingast 1987; Weingast and Marshall 1988; Gilligan, Marshall, and Weingast 1989; and others explore how legislative institutions alter political outcomes. For a more thorough survey of the new institutional economics, see Eggertsson 1990.

Chapter 2

1. The data on physical capital are from U.S. Department of Interior 1894, 768–75. This is part II of the compendium to the eleventh census. The data on total output in the city and in individual industries are from U.S. Department of the Interior 1895, xxxii–xxxv. This is the eleventh census, manufacturing industries, statistics of cities. I use the census measure "gross value product." See also Pierce 1957, 155, 223.

2. See citations in note 1 to this chapter.

3. For investments in gas mains, see Chicago City Council 1906, 21. For main life, see Chicago City Council 1906, 14. For current dollar estimates of costs of gas mains, I use the following data. In 1991, the general price level was about fifteen times greater than it was during the early 1890s. See McCusker 1992, 329–32. Also, according the Illinois Bureau of Labor Statistics, it cost $9,000 to install a single mile of gas mains during the early 1890s. See Illinois Bureau of Labor Statistics 1897, 304.

4. See Nisbet-Latta 1907, 141–50, and Forestall 1920, 51–52, 74–75, 81–83, 162–64, 216–18, 253–54.

5. For relative costs of mains and plants I used the following data. Richards 1877, 335, presents data indicating that during the mid-nineteenth century the construction of a single large gas plant cost about £14,000. Assuming that it cost £396 to lay one mile of gas mains, five hundred miles of mains cost £198,000. The assumption that it cost £396 to lay one mile of gas mains translates into a cost of 4.5 shillings per yard. According to the data presented in Richards 1877, 260, this is a lower bound estimate of the costs of main construction. For plant life, see Chicago City Council 1906, 15–17.

6. For rule governing immediate and delayed relief, see *William R. Wilcox v. Consolidated Gas Company of New York,* 29 S.Crt. 192 (1908) and *Des Moines Gas Company v. City of Des Moines,* 35 S. Crt. 811 (1914). For the quotation, see McCurdy 1925, 224. See also Hovenkamp 1988.

7. *Louisville Gas Co. v. Citizens' Gas-Light Co.,* 115 U.S. 683 (1885), especially 699–700. See also *New Orleans Gas Light Co. v. Louisiana Light & Heat Producing & Manuf'g Co. and others,* 115 U.S. 650 (1885).

8. For low taxes paid by Chicago utilities, see Nord 1979, 63–67. For ability to sue if rates exceeded those dictated by franchise, see, for example, *Pingree v. Mutual Gas Co.,* 65 N.W. 6 (1895). Chapter 4 considers the case in detail. For decisions on fixed charges and meter rents, see, for example, *Louisville Gas Co. v. Dulaney, et al.,* 38 S.W. 703 (1897) and *Village of Otsego v. Allegan County Gas Co.,* 168 N.W. 968 (1918).

9. For Cleveland franchise, see Wilcox 1910, 599–601. For gas rates in Cleveland, see 1887 volume of *Brown's Directory of American Gas Companies.*

10. Wilcox 1910, 573, 582.

11. See Olson's 1965 classic exposition of the theory.

12. See Gilligan, Marshall, and Weingast 1989 for a more developed analysis of the multiple interest group perspective.

13. In arguing that the courts were endogenous, I am not breaking new ground. See, for example, Rutten's 1991 analysis of the courts during the late nineteenth and early twentieth centuries. See also Gely and Spiller 1990 for a formal treatment of the courts in political context. See, more generally, Posner 1994 and Rasmussen 1994.

14. This discussion of the Illinois judiciary is drawn from Fiedler 1973, 228–30.

Chapter 3

1. For the founding of the gas industry in America, see Stotz and Jamison 1938, 5–9. For percentage of coal gas used for lighting in 1890, see U.S. Department of Interior 1895, 706. For the cost of lighting a home, I perform the following calculation. It required about two thousand cubic feet of gas to light the typical household for a month. During the early 1870s, gas (in Chicago) sold for $3.50 per MCF. The average U.S. laborer earned roughly $480 per year in 1870. These estimates use data from the following sources: *Chicago Tribune,* June 8, 1888, 8; Peoples Gas Light and Coke Company 1900; U.S. Department of Commerce 1975, 165; and Lebergott 1976, 346–47. For patterns of gas use in Chicago before 1880, see Platt 1991, 14. For changes in gas lighting and comparisons of gas with other lighting technologies, see *Engineering News,* March 19, 1892, 274; Lebergott 1993, 119–21; Platt 1991, 1–40; Rose 1995, 27–30; and U.S. Department of the Interior 1902, 713. For patterns of gas usage, see Lebergott 1993, table II.21, 120, and Lebergott 1976, 347.

2. For the superiority of electricity as a lighting source, see Gould 1946, 86, and Lebergott 1993, 120. For the percentage of gas used for illumination in 1919, see Passer 1953, 199. For data on when families began using electricity to heat their homes, see Lebergott 1993, 107. See Illinois General Assembly 1917, 7, for the data on gas and electric consumers. This state report did not specify if by "gas consumers" it referred to natural or manufactured gas. However, a thorough survey of the financial statements of the Peoples Gas Light and Coke Company (the city's

only gas provider) over this period suggest that the company produced and sold coal gas almost exclusively. See also Stotz and Jamison 1938, 297; Gould 1946, 89–95; and Lebergott 1993, table II.21, 120.

3. A full copy of the Chicago Gas Light and Coke Company's charter can be found in Illinois Bureau of Labor Statistics 1897, 239. For information on the Peoples Gas Company, see Illinois Bureau of Labor Statistics 1897, 240–41, and Pierce 1957, 320–21.

4. For general outlines of the history of the Chicago gas industry from its inception until the early 1880s, see the following sources: Illinois Bureau of Labor Statistics 1897, 276–79; Chicago City Council 1914, 19–20; Rice 1925, 1–33; and Smith 1926, 10–20.

5. Throughout the 1850s and 1860s, engineers had been experimenting with water gas. However, it was not until Thaddeus C. Lowe patented the process described later in this chapter that water gas production became commercially attractive. See Shelton 1889, 192.

6. On comparative lighting power, a survey of nearly eight hundred gas companies operating in 1894 indicates that the average candle power of water gas was more than twenty-five while the average candle power of ordinary coal gas was less than nineteen. The survey of candle power is constructed from data found in *Brown's Directory of American Gas Companies.* The data are available from the author upon request. See the following sources for more general statements on the superior lighting power of water gas: U.S. Department of the Interior 1902, 711; Rice 1925, 34–35; and American Gas, Fuel and Light Company 1881. For water gas economizing on labor, see *Engineering News,* May 30, 1891, 513. Chicago gas companies actually began manufacturing water gas, in part, because of the "expensive labor troubles" they faced with coal gas. See Chicago City Council 1906, 10. Also, the United Gas Improvement Company (1911, 17) claimed that "Water gas manufacture requires much less labor than coal gas manufacture." For other statements on labor costs in water gas plants, see U.S. Department of the Interior, 1902, 711, and Rice 1925, 34. For statements on relative (capital) costs of coal and water gas plants, see Chicago City Council 1906, 10, and United Gas Improvement Company 1911, 15. For water gas plant built in old church, see Shelton 1889, 194.

7. See Shelton 1889, 192, U.S. Department of the Interior 1895, 706, and U.S. Department of the Interior 1902, 711.

8. For the chemical makeup of gas, see Wood 1877, 6. For the antiwater-gas law, see Pratt 1885, 7. See also U.S. Department of the Interior 1902, 714; American Gas, Fuel and Light Company 1881, 1–4; and Shelton 1889.

9. See Wood 1877, 2–5, 7.

10. The Consumers Gas Company produced water gas. See the following issues of *American Gas Light Journal:* August 16, 1883, 81; April 16, 1885, 209; and June 16, 1885, 320. Also, the 1887 volume of *Brown's Directory of American Gas Companies* reported that the Equitable Gas Light and Fuel Company, the Consumers Gas, Fuel and Light Company, the Chicago Gas Light and Coke Company, and the Peoples Gas Light and Coke Company all produced water gas. Data are not available for the other Chicago gas companies. For more details on the Consumers Gas Company, see Illinois Bureau of Labor Statistics 1897, 277, and Chicago City Council 1914, 19.

11. See Illinois Bureau of Labor Statistics 1897, 276–78; Chicago City Council 1914, 19; and Rice 1925, 20–37.

12. See Platt 1991, 47, and Rice 1925, 35.

13. For Equitable's troubles, see *Commercial and Financial Chronicle,* December 15, 1888, 746. For the behavior of stock prices, see various issues of the *Chicago Tribune* or *Commercial and Financial Chronicle.*

14. See *Chicago Gas Light Co. v. Peoples Gas Light Co.,* 121 Ill. 530 (1887). For the quotations, see pages 544–55 of the decision.

15. See the following sources: Rice 1925, 30–31; Illinois Bureau of Labor Statistics 1897, 277–78; and *Chicago Tribune,* August 6, 1885, 8. Also see the following issues of *American Gas Light Journal,* April 16, 1885, 209; June 16, 1885, 320; August 2, 1886, 78; December 16, 1886, 364–65; and March 2, 1887, 130. For the quotations, see *Commercial and Financial Chronicle,* December 15, 1888, 746.

16. Stock prices are from the *Chicago Tribune* and the following issues of *American Gas Light Journal:* October 16, 1886, 240, and December 16, 1886, 368.

17. See Illinois Bureau of Labor Statistics 1897, 304–5; Chicago City Council 1914, 22, and Chicago City Council 1906, 1. See the following issues of the *Chicago Tribune:* March 23, 1893, 1, 12, and October 7, 1894, 3–4. Finally, see the following issues of *American Gas Light Journal:* September 10, 1894, 409, and September 24, 1894, 444.

18. See *Chicago Tribune,* February 22, 1892, 1, and *New York Times,* May 11, 1890, 5, and July 12, 1890, 8.

19. The story of the Ogden Gas Company is well known to Chicago historians. For secondary accounts that agree with the extortion or boodle interpretation, see, for example, Ginger 1958, 172–74; Tarr 1966; and Tarr 1971, 75, 79–80, 87. For an interpretation that claims the Ogden's backers had intended all along to create a competing firm, see Barnard 1938, 406–10. For accounts from the Chicago press, see, for example, the following issues of the *Chicago Tribune:* March 4, 1895, 1, 2, 6; March 5, 1895, 1, 11; and March 6, 1895, 4. (The *Tribune* claimed that the ordinance was intended to blackmail the gas trust.) See also Illinois Bureau of Labor Statistics 1897, 306; Chicago City Council 1914, 22; and Harrison 1935, 193.

20. See the following issues of *American Gas Light Journal:* June 5, 1893, 157; August 27, 1894, 301; and March 12, 1895, 336.

21. This brief synopsis of the Atlanta gas industry is taken from Tate 1985, 1–40.

22. The story of New York's gas situation is taken from Stotz and Jamison 1938, 20–66; information on prices is gathered from *Brown's Directory of American Gas Companies.* For other cities, see *Brown's Directory of American Gas Companies* 1887, 85–89; Brown 1936; Wilcox 1910; Shelton 1889; and the following issues of *American Gas Light Journal:* August 2, 1879, 49; October 16, 1879, 169; October 16, 1884, 207; and November 3, 1884, 236. Court reporters provide another source of information.

Chapter 4

1. After the Chicago Gas Trust Company increased its rates on the city's north and south sides, the *Tribune* surveyed one thousand Chicagoans about their opin-

ions of gas service in the city. According to the survey, north and south side consumers were "unanimous" in their dissatisfaction with the gas trust (*Chicago Tribune,* January 8, 1888, 9). It was this sort of dissatisfaction that motivated the citizen's association. See Chicago Citizen's Association 1888, 8–10; Chicago Citizen's Association 1889, 8; Nord 1979, 38–40, 44, 46, 54, 62; and Pierce 1957, 222.

2. A few members of the citizen's association held a financial interest in the gas trust. These members opposed the suit against the gas trust. For example, C. Norman Faye, a member of the citizen's association and an officer of the gas trust, tried to dissuade Peabody from sponsoring the suit. See Hunt 1890, 34–41; Faye 1909; and the following issues of the *Chicago Tribune:* February 3, 1888, 6; February 7, 1888, 6; and February 8, 1888, 1.

3. For a general statement, see Hovenkamp 1991, 57. For some actual cases, consider the following. Illinois and Nebraska brought suits against the whiskey trust, eventually leading the combination to organize as a New Jersey holding company; see *The Distilling and Cattle Feeding Co. v. The People ex. rel.,* 157 Ill. 448 (1895) and *State v. Nebraska Distilling Company, et al.,* 29 Neb. 700 (1890). Missouri and Ohio attacked Standard Oil through quo warranto proceedings; see *State v. Standard Oil Co.,* 49 Ohio St. 137, 182 (1892) and *State ex inf. v. Standard Oil Co.,* 217–18 Mo. 1 (1908). The sugar trust was involved in litigation in California and New York; see *People v. The American Sugar Refining Company,* 7 Ry. & Corp. L.J. 83 (1890) and *People v. North River Sugar Refining Company,* 121 N.Y. 582 (1890). Missouri employed a quo warranto proceeding to oust the meatpacking trust from the state; see *The State v. Armour Packing Co.,* 173 Mo. 356 (1902).

4. See the following issues of the *Chicago Tribune:* May 22, 1889, 3, and May 23, 1889, 5.

5. For stock prices and market reaction, see *Chicago Tribune:* November 28, 1889, 1, 2, 12; November 30, 1889, 1; and December 1, 1889, 12. For the court's decision and quotations, see *People v. Chicago Gas Trust Company,* 130 Ill. 268 1889, 292–93.

6. See the following issues of *Commercial and Financial Chronicle:* March 3, 1890, 352; March 22, 1890, 422; April 5, 1890, 487; May 31, 1890, 770; and June 28, 1890, 904.

7. The quotations and information in this paragraph are taken from the following sources: *People v. Chicago Gas Trust Company,* 130 Ill. 268 (1889), 292, and *New York Times,* September 23, 1890, 2; November 9, 1890, 9; and April 24, 1890, 1. See also the following issues of *Commercial and Financial Chronicle:* November 8, 1890, 645, and November 15, 1890, 680.

8. The paper wrote: "The only other plan that has yet been discussed is the organization of a bona fide, out and out trust. Some good lawyers . . . claim that this plan presents no legal obstacles that cannot be surmounted." See *Chicago Tribune,* November 30, 1889, 1. See also the following issues of *Commercial and Financial Chronicle:* November 8, 1890, 645; November 15, 1890, 680; and January 24, 1891, 164.

9. For a description of this new trust arrangement see *Commercial and Financial Chronicle,* December 19, 1891, 921, and *American Gas Light Journal,* June 29, 1891, 927.

10. Illinois Bureau of Labor Statistics 1897, 287.

11. For New Jersey chartermongering, see Grandy 1989. For trusts reorganizing in New Jersey to avoid state antitrust enforcement, see Hovenkamp 1991, 258.

12. All the information about the New Jersey Gas Act is taken from two court cases: *State, Richards, et al., Prosecutors v. Mayor, Etc., of Dover et al.,* 61 N.J.L. 400 (1898) and *The Jersey City Gas Company v. George S. Dwight and others,* 29 N.J. Eq. 243 (1878).

13. See *The Jersey City Gas Company v. George S. Dwight and others,* 29 N.J. Eq. 243 (1878) and *State, Richards, et al., Prosecutors v. Mayor, Etc., of Dover et al.,* 61 N.J.L. 400 (1898).

14. See *Seattle Gas & Electric Co. v. Citizens' Light & Power Co.,* 123 Fed. 588 (1903).

15. See the following sources on the legal battles between the city and the Economic Company: Chicago City Council 1914, 22; *Chicago Tribune,* March 2, 1892, 4; Illinois Bureau of Labor Statistics 1897, 289; and *American Gas Light Journal,* March 14, 1892, 373. For the consumer response to the trust's acquisition of the Economic Company, see *Chicago Tribune,* February 27, 1892, 2, and February 25, 1892, 1.

16. For the attorney general's suit, see the following issues of the *Chicago Tribune:* April 19, 1894, 4; April 24, 1894, 4; April 25, 1894, 1- 2, 4, 6; April 26, 1894, 5; and May 12, 1894, 11. For market response and other information, see *American Gas Light Journal,* July 9, 1894, 49; *Chicago Tribune,* July 3, 1894, 4; and Illinois Bureau of Labor Statistics 1897, 293–94, 309.

17. For the interview with the company's attorney, see *Chicago Tribune,* July 19, 1894, 7. For details on the reorganization plan and its reception, see the following issues of *American Gas Light Journal:* October 7, 1895, 578; October 14, 1895, 616–17, and October 21, 1895, 658. For the market's response to the plan, see the following issues of the *Chicago Tribune:* September 25, 1895, 11, and October 5, 1895, 2.

18. See *City of Detroit v. Mutual Gas Company,* 6 N.W. 1039 (1880) and Holli 1969, 87.

19. See Holli 1969, 86–94, and *Pingree v. Mutual Gas Co.,* 65 N.W. 6 (1895).

20. For New York, see the following issues of the *New York Times:* January 30, 1885, 2; January 31, 1885, 2; February 7, 1885, 5; February 15, 1885, 2; March 31, 1885, 2; April 5, 1885, 4; May 14, 1885, 2; November 24, 1885, 3; November 26, 1885, 8; December 3, 1885, 8; December 4, 1885, 8; December 18, 1885, 8; December 19, 1885, 5; December 22, 1885, 3; December 31, 1885, 8; May 5, 1886, 4; June 14, 1886, 8; June 15, 1886, 8; July 27, 1886, 1; November 4, 1886, 2; and November 14, 1886, 14. For Baltimore, see Brown 1936. For Peoria, see the discussion and citations that conclude the chapter on municipal regulation. For St. Louis, see *State ex. rel. City of St. Louis v. Laclede Gas Light Co.,* 14 S.W. 974 (1890) and *New York Times,* April 19, 1890, 2.

21. Economists often argue that antitrust regulation is intended to protect small firms from their larger, more efficient competitors. See, for example, Libecap 1992 and Stigler 1985.

Chapter 5

1. See *American Gas Light Journal,* March 25, 1895, 413, and *Chicago Tribune,* June 25, 1895, 3.

2. The provisions of the consolidation act are set out in *The People ex. rel. Charles Deneen v. The Peoples Gas Light and Coke Company,* 205 Ill. 482 (1903). For the frontage act, see Chicago City Council 1914, 22.

3. See a pamphlet published by a group called the Bi-Partisan Alliance titled "The Public Records Concerning Sullivan and Sherman," (n.d.). It is available at the Chicago Historical Society. The pamphlet includes excerpts from several newspapers regarding the gas acts. See also *Chicago Tribune,* May 20, 1897, 2, 7; Tarr 1966, 457; and Tarr 1971, 79–80.

4. See Civic Federation of Chicago 1897, 3, and *Chicago Tribune,* May 28, 1897, 2, and June 2, 1897, 2. Pegram (1992) writes that "a coalition of businesspeople, professionals, labor leaders and social workers created the Civic Federation." He adds that after its founding in 1893, "[b]usinesspeople and professionals quickly came to dominate the federation . . . turning it to the middle-class purposes of cleaning up city hall and promoting efficiency in the conduct of public business" (Pegram 1992, 91). See also Roberts 1960.

5. See *Journal of the Senate of the Fortieth General Assembly of the State of Illinois* 1897, 600–601, 700–701, 744–45, 780–81, 788–89, 794–95, 822–23. See also *Chicago Tribune,* May 20, 1897, 9.

6. The outline here is from various issues of *Commercial and Financial Chronicle;* Chicago City Council 1914, 20–22; Rice 1925, 37–43; and *Peoples Gas Light and Coke Co. v. Frederick C. Hale, et al.,* 94 Ill. App. 406 (1900).

7. For the relationship between the Municipal and Peoples companies, see *Chicago Tribune,* September 26, 1900, 9. See Burns 1986 and Tenant 1950 for a detailed discussion of predatory pricing by American Tobacco. In a well-known article, McGee 1958 takes issue with the claim that Standard Oil used predatory pricing. Gabel (1994) explores the predatory techniques used by AT&T at the turn of the century.

8. See the following issues of the *Chicago Tribune:* September 2, 1900, 7; September 9, 1900, 13; and September 12, 1900, 7. See also the following issues of *Commercial and Financial Chronicle:* September 8, 1900, 506; December 11, 1897, 1116; April 7, 1900, 692; April 21, 1900, 798; October 13, 767; and October 20, 1900, 817.

9. See Bi-Partisan Alliance (n.d.), 17, which includes excerpts from the *Chicago Economist* describing the contract between Hamilton and the Ogden. The following issues of *Commercial and Financial Chronicle* are also used: October 20, 1900, 817; November 10, 1900, 970; December 15, 1900; and January 12, 1901, 91.

10. See the annual report of the Peoples Gas Light and Coke Company for the year ending 1913.

11. See the following issues of the *Chicago Tribune:* September 12, 1900, 7; September 27, 1900, 2; September 25, 1900, 1–2; September 28, 1900, 1–3; and September 29, 1900, 4.

12. See Bi-Partisan Alliance (n.d.), 18–24, which reprints several court-filed affidavits describing Sullivan's role in organizing the consumer protest meeting.

13. For Darrow's speech, see *Chicago Tribune,* September 28, 1900, 1–3. For other details, see Bi-Partisan Alliance (n.d.), 18–23.

14. See *The People ex. rel. v. Peoples Gas Light and Coke Co.,* 205 Ill. 482 (1903) and the following issues of the *Chicago Tribune:* October 28, 1903, 5, and September 8, 1900, 8.

15. See Ginger 1958 and Tierney's 1979 biography of Darrow, especially 73–74, 76, 117, 119, 162–63, 165, 167, 171–72, . For Sullivan, see, for example, McCaffrey et al. 1987, 64, 68–69, 78–79, 93. For a less generous view of Darrow, see Cowan 1993.

16. According to the *Tribune,* "gas and questions raised by the existing gas war on the North Side took up all of the time" at the council's first fall meeting. See *Chicago Tribune,* September 25, 1900, 1.

17. See *Chicago Tribune,* October 16, 1900, 2, and September 29, 1900, 4.

18. See *Chicago Tribune,* October 16, 1900, 1, and *Peoples Gas Light and Coke Company v. City of Chicago,* 48 L. Ed. 851 (1903).

19. Quotations from *Mills v. City of Chicago, et al.,* 127 Fed. 731 (1904), 731. See also *City of Chicago v. Darius O. Mills,* 51 L. Ed. 504 (1907).

20. See *Chicago Tribune,* June 8, 1897, 6. For the details of Magruder's legal career, see Palmer 1899, 66–69.

21. See *Chicago Record-Herald,* April 27, 1906, 5, and the following issues of the *Chicago American:* May 29, 1906, and May 30, 1906.

22. See *Chicago Record-Herald,* May 15, 1906; *Chicago American,* May 29, 1906, and May 30, 1906; and *Chicago Tribune,* June 5, 1906, 1. For life expectancy, see Fogel 1986.

23. See *Chicago Record-Herald,* April 26, 1906, 5, and May 16, 1906. See also *Chicago Tribune,* June 5, 1906, 1, and June 8, 1897, 2.

24. *Chicago Tribune,* February 12, 1906, 6.

25. For the discussion of Cleveland, see Van Tassel and Grabowski 1987, 356–57. For the discussion of Cincinnati, see Miller 1968, 170–71. For the discussion of AT&T, see Gabel 1994, 562–63.

Chapter 6

1. See *Chicago Record-Herald,* April 27, 1905, 2, and April 21, 1905, 4. In addition, see *Chicago Tribune,* April 7, 1905, and April 26, 1905, 4.

2. Meagher's quotations are from the *Chicago Tribune,* April 28, 1905, 6. Sullivan's quotations are from the *Chicago Tribune,* April 27, 1905, 7. Also, according to the *Record-Herald,* officials of Peoples Gas also met privately with various representatives and the governor to protest the passage of municipal regulation laws. See *Chicago Record-Herald,* April 26, 1905, 1, and April 27, 1905, 2.

3. The *Tribune* (April 27, 1905, 1) reported: "[the state regulation] measure receives the full and hearty support of the gas companies, big and little. The small

manufacturers from down the state are working for it energetically and the large companies of Chicago will 'accept' it if they have to 'accept' anything."

4. See the following issues of the *Chicago Tribune:* April 26, 1905, 4; April 27, 1905, 1; and April 24, 1905, 1, 4. And see *Chicago Record-Herald,* April 26, 1905, 1.

5. For legislative history of the Enabling Act, see the following issues of the *Chicago Tribune:* April 7, 1905, 7; April 12, 1905, 5; April 13, 1905, 5; April 20, 1905, 1–2; April 22, 1905, 5; April 23, 1905, 5; April 24, 1905, 4; April 25, 1905, 4; April 26, 1905, 1, 4; April 27, 1905, 1, 7; April 28, 1905, 1, 6; April 29, 1905, 4; April 30, 1905, 8; May 2, 1905, 4; May 3, 1905, 1, 4; May 4, 1905, 1, 4; May 5, 1905, 1, 4, 6; May 6, 1905, 1, 4; May 7, 1905, 1, 4; and May 8, 1905, 6. In addition, see the following issues of the *Chicago Record-Herald:* April 13, 1905, 1; April 20, 1905, 1; April 21, 1905, 1, 4; April 26, 1905, 1; April 27, 1905, 2; April 28, 1905, 4; May 2, 1905, 1, 4; May 3, 1905, 1, 4; and May 19, 1905, 3.

6. See, for example, *Chicago Record-Herald,* May 19, 1905, 1, and *Commercial and Financial Chronicle,* May 13, 1905, 1916. The constitutional questions centered around how the act was titled and the act's liberal delegation of regulatory authority to the city (*Chicago Tribune,* May 6, 1905, 4, and May 7, 1905, 4). By 1914, even the legal counsel for the City of Chicago conceded that the constitutionality of the Enabling Act "is in the gravest doubt" (*Opinions of the Corporation Counsel and Assistants,* January 1, 1913, to October 5, 1914). These doubts proved accurate; see subsequent discussion in the text.

7. See Buenker 1995.

8. Morton 1990, 221; Buenker 1995, 41; McCaffrey et al. 1987, 67.

9. For the council's refusal to confirm Finerty, see *Chicago Tribune,* December 19, 1906, 6. For other issues, see Buenker 1995 and McCaffrey et al. 1987, 66–67. Note that Buenker and McCaffrey et al. stress that Dunne realized greater success when he did not have to deal with the city council.

10. See the following issues of the *Chicago Tribune:* November 14, 1905, 1, and November 28, 1905, 2. See also *Chicago Record-Herald,* November 20, 1905. The *Record-Herald* citation is from a volume of newspaper clippings on Chicago's gas situation found at the Chicago Historical Society. Hereafter, I will refer to these clippings by citing the newspaper's name and simply "clippings."

11. Meagher's quotation is from the *Chicago Tribune,* December 8, 1905, 1. The quotation on dividends is also from the *Tribune,* December 20, 1905, 3. Other information is taken from the following issues of the *Chicago Tribune:* December 7, 1905, 2; November 25, 1905, 2; and September 30, 1910, 15.

12. For a biography of Bemis, see Holmgren 1964. The discussion of Bemis and the quotation are taken from Holmgren 1964, 107, 316. For the council's decision to begin investigating, see various Chicago papers of December 6, 1905, found in newspaper clippings at the Chicago Historical Society.

13. See Chicago City Council 1906, 3, and the following issues of the *Chicago Tribune:* December 9, 1905, 6; January 25, 1906, 1; and January 30, 1906, 4. For Cowdery's position in 1906, see Chicago City Council 1906. For Cowdery's association with the Peoples Gas Company in subsequent years, see the annual reports of the Peoples Gas Light and Coke Company, 1908 through 1920.

14. The Bemis and Humphreys quotations are from Chicago City Council 1906, 4, 26, respectively.

15. Quoted in *Chicago Tribune,* December 30, 1905, 7. See Chicago City Council 1906, 44, 49, for the recommendations of Cowdery and Humphreys. See *Chicago Tribune,* January 25, 1906, 1, and December 30, 1905, 7, for Bemis's recommendations.

16. See *Chicago Tribune,* January 30, 1906, 4, and February 9, 1906, 1, 4.

17. Incidentally, the *Tribune* (February 11, 1906, 5) reported: "The mayor received an anonymous letter . . . warning him that if he did not veto the 85-cent gas ordinance, Mrs. Dunne will be a widow in thirty days." Signed with a skull and crossbones, the mayor did not take the letter too seriously. He laughed and filed it in an appropriate place. For other matters, see the following issues of the *Tribune:* February 10, 1906, 1; February 11, 1906, 5; February 13, 1906, 3; February 15, 1906, 2; and February 16, 1906, 6.

18. See *Chicago Tribune,* December 1, 1910, 4, and December 23, 1910, 17. See also the following papers: *Chicago Examiner,* December 1, 1910; December 9, 1910; March 31, 1911; and April 2, 1911 (all in clippings) and *Chicago American,* December 10, 1910 (clippings).

19. See Kantowicz 1995 and *Chicago Tribune,* January 9, 1911, 4.

20. All of Graham's quotations are from the *Chicago Tribune,* January 9, 1911, 4. See McCaffrey et al. 1987, 67–68, for a general discussion of the primary. See also McCarthy 1974.

21. *Chicago Tribune,* March 30, 1911, 4.

22. On party defections generally, see Ickes 1943, 129–44; Kantowicz 1995; Kantowicz 1975, 77–83; McCaffrey et al. 1987, 68; and Merriam 1929, 279–86. See Ickes 1943, 132–33, for a description of Sullivan's antics. Merriam 1929, 284, denies consenting to Sullivan's support. A wonderful description of the campaign can also be found in the *New York Times* (April 2, 1911, pt. 6, 11): "It happened that when Mr. Dunne ran for mayor in 1905, Mr. Harrison went to California and did not return until election day. Now Mr. Dunne has found it necessary to take a rest and he will remain at the springs of Michigan until April 4 and will not be able to help Mr. Harrison in the campaign."

23. See Kantowicz 1975, 83, and Kantowicz 1995, 29.

24. See *Chicago Tribune,* April 5, 1911, 5, and *Commercial and Financial Chronicle,* April 8, 1911, 960. The event study results are available from the author upon request.

25. *Chicago Tribune,* March 28, 1911, 4–10.

26. See Holmgren 1964, 317; *Chicago Tribune,* April 19, 1911, 9; and *Chicago Record Herald,* April 20, 1911, 1.

27. See *Chicago Tribune,* April 20, 1911, 1. For all the quotations from the *Chicago Examiner,* see Holmgren 1964, 317–18.

28. See *Chicago Examiner,* June 10, 1911, and *Chicago Record-Herald,* June 10, 1911 (both in clippings).

29. See Bemis 1911, especially 5–7, 12–13.

30. See Bemis 1911, 14, 30; *Chicago Record-Herald,* July 18, 1911, 1; and Holmgren 1964, 319.

31. See *City of Chicago v. The Peoples Gas Light and Coke Company,* 170 Ill. App. 98 (1912), 104–5, for the quotations. See the annual report of the Peoples Gas Light and Coke Company, December, 1911, 4–5, for a more accessible overview of the court battles. See also Weber 1919.

32. See *City of Chicago v. The Peoples Gas Light and Coke Company,* 170 Ill. App. 98 (1912), 110–11, for the quotations.

33. See *Sutter v. Peoples Gas Light and Coke Co.,* 284 Ill. 634 (1918), 646, and *Mills v. Peoples Gas Light and Coke Co.,* 327 Ill. 508 (1927).

34. For the calculation putting Bemis's bill in current dollars, the general price level in 1992 was about fourteen greater than it had been in 1911. See McCusker 1992, 330–32, "Consumer Composite Price Index." For Bemis's bill to the city, see *Chicago Tribune,* July 22, 1911 (clippings). For Bemis's role in Des Moines and Omaha rate cases, see the following issues of the *Chicago Record-Herald:* July 20, 1911; September 22, 1911; and September 23, 1911 (clippings).

35. Quotations from Holmgren 1964, 247, 311.

36. See Hoyt 1933, 493. For a thorough analysis of the development of Chicago's electric industry, see Platt 1991.

37. From a speech delivered before the Pacific Gas Association at its annual convention in the fall of 1908. The speech was reprinted in *American Gas Light Journal,* September 28, 1908, 527.

38. McDonald 1957, 117. See also McDonald's 1962 biography of Samuel Insull.

39. See the following issues of the *Cleveland Leader and Herald:* May 5, 1891, 8; August 11, 1891, 8; August 12, 1891, 5; August 25, 1891, 8; August 28, 1891, 8; November 14, 1891, 8; and June 1, 1892, 1.

40. In its decision, the court said it was following the doctrine of the *Reagan* cases, a doctrine the court described as "very well understood and familiar." See *New Memphis Gas & Light Company v. City of Memphis,* 72 Fed. 952 (1896), 956.

41. Peoria's narrative is taken from the court decision and the following issues of the *Peoria Herald-Transcript:* August 1, 1900, 8; August 4, 1900, 8; August 7, 1900, 8; August 9, 1900, 4; September 5, 1900, 8; April 19, 1905, 1; April 20, 1905, 8; April 25, 1905, 7; and May 5, 1905, 8.

42. See *Peoria Herald-Transcript,* January 3, 1906, 12.

43. The Court explained: "Parties making an agreement, unlawful by the antitrust act, may, while the agreement is in force, be subject to its penalties; but, whenever they cease to act under it, the penalties also cease. The punishment adheres to the offense, and stops when the offense itself stops." See *Peoria Gas & Electric Company v. City of Peoria,* 26 S.Crt. 214 (1906), 216.

Chapter 7

1. See Illinois General Assembly 1913, 855–59, and Illinois General Assembly 1917. See also Kneier 1927, 158, who writes: "The general sentiment in Chicago was opposed to state regulation; the opinion expressed . . . being that control

should be vested in the local authorities." For voters in Springfield, see *Springfield Illinois State Register,* June 23, 1913, 4.

2. See Illinois General Assembly 1913, 857.

3. Illinois General Assembly 1913, 857; and see Wendt and Kogan 1943, 172–73.

4. All quotations are from Illinois General Assembly 1913, 860–61.

5. See the following issues of the *Chicago Tribune:* June 13, 1913, 2; June 15, 1913, 2; and June 21, 1913, 1–2.

6. See *Springfield Illinois State Register,* June 23, 1913, 4, and *Chicago Tribune,* June 14, 1913, 2.

7. See the following issues of the *Chicago Tribune:* June 24, 1913, 1–2, and June 25, 1913, 1.

8. See the following issues of the *Chicago Tribune:* June 24, 1913, 1–2; June 25, 1913, 1; June 26, 1913, 1–2; June 27, 1913, 1; June 28, 1913, 1–2; July 1913, 1, 7; and July 2, 1913, 1. See also *Quincy Daily Herald,* June 25, 1913, 1.

9. See *Chicago Tribune,* June 21, 1913, 1, and July 1, 1913, 6.

10. The returns of the Peoples Gas Company are calculated using an average of the daily high and low price because the *Chronicle* does not report closing prices. Also, the *New York Times,* the only other reliable contemporary source of stock price data, did not regularly report the closing price of the Peoples Gas Company during this period.

11. See the annual reports of the Peoples Gas Light and Coke Company for 1917 and 1918 and the following issues of the *Commercial and Financial Chronicle:* March 16, 1918, 1132; March 23, 1918, 1235; April 27, 1918, 1800; and May 25, 1918, 2233–34. For details on state regulation from 1919 through 1922, see the following issues of the *Commercial and Financial Chronicle:* February 8, 1919, 586; February 15, 1919, 679; March 22, 1919, 1170; May 24, 1919, 2129; June 21, 1919, 2533; July 12, 1919, 179; August 2, 1919, 483; May 1, 1920, 1856; June 19, 1920, 2573; August 7, 1920, 596; September 25, 1920, 1285; November 27, 1920, 2145; January 15, 1921, 265; April 23, 1921, 1747; April 30, 1921, 1874; January 14, 1922, 205; and February 18, 1922, 745.

12. Quoted in Illinois General Assembly 1917, 27. To the degree that legislatures anticipated administrative shirking and devised procedural rules to minimize it, this problem would have been limited. See McCubbins, Noll, and Weingast 1989. Shepsle 1992 provides some reasons why it might be difficult to forestall all administrative shirking, or what he and others call bureaucratic drift.

13. See Illinois General Assembly 1917 for a more detailed description of this attempt to amend the IPUA.

14. See Kneier 1927.

15. Quoted in *Chicago Tribune,* April 26, 1905, 4.

16. See Von Sinderen 1906 and discussion of first *Mills* decision. See also my discussion in chapter 1.

17. For Ohio's battle over public utility regulation, see the following issues of the *Cleveland Plain Dealer:* May 5, 1911, 1; May 10, 1911, 1; May 12, 1911, 6; May 26,

1911, 6; May 27, 1911, 5; and May 31, 1911, 13. In addition, see the following issues of the *Cleveland Press:* April 6, 1910, 9; May 12, 1911, 13; May 13, 1911, 4; May 25, 1911, 1; May 27, 1911, 2; May 31, 1911, 1–2; and June 1, 1911, 1. For the quotations and other information on California utilities, see Blackford 1977, 87–88. See also Minnesota Home Rule League (1914).

References

American Gas, Fuel and Light Company. 1881. Facts, Not Fancies, Regarding Water Gas. New York: American Gas, Fuel and Light Company.

American Gas Light Journal. Various issues, 1880–1915.

Andreas, A. T. 1975. *History of Chicago from the Earliest Period to the Present Time in Three Volumes.* New York: Arno Press.

Barnard, Harry. 1938. *Eagle Forgotten: The Life of John Peter Altgeld.* New York: Duell, Sloan and Pearce.

Bemis, Edward W. 1911. *Report upon the Price of Gas in Chicago for the Chicago City Council Committee on Gas, Oil and Electric Light.* Chicago: Henry O. Shepard Company.

Binder, John J. 1988. The Sherman Antitrust Act and the Railroad Cartels. *Journal of Law and Economics* 31:443–68.

———. 1985. Measuring the Effects of Regulation with Stock Price Data. *Rand Journal of Economics* 16:167–83.

Bi-Partisan Alliance. N.d. *The Public Records Concerning Sullivan and Sherman.* Twenty-five page pamphlet found at the Chicago Historical Society. No publisher.

Blackford, Mansel G. 1977. *The Politics of Business in California, 1890–1920.* Columbus: Ohio State University Press.

———. 1970. Businessmen and the Regulation of Railroads and Public Utilities in California during the Progressive Era. *Business History Review* 44:7–19.

Brown, George T. 1936. *The Gas Light Company of Baltimore: A Study of Natural Monopoly.* Baltimore: Johns Hopkins University Press.

Brown, Stephen, and Jerold Warner. 1985. Using Daily Stock Returns: The Case of Event Studies. *Journal of Financial Economics* 24:3–31.

Brown's Directory of American Gas Companies. New York: Progressive Age. Various years, 1887–1924.

Buenker, John D. 1995. Edward F. Dunne: The Limits of Municipal Reform. In *The Mayors: The Chicago Political Tradition,* 33–49. Edited by Paul M. Green and Melvin G. Holli. Carbondale: Southern Illinois University Press.

Burns, Malcolm. 1986. Predatory Pricing and the Acquisition Cost of Competitors. *Journal of Political Economy* 94:266–96.

Chandler, Alfred D. 1977. *The Visible Hand: The Managerial Revolution in American Business.* Cambridge, MA: Harvard University Press.

Chicago American. Various issues and clippings files regarding Chicago gas matters. Chicago Historical Society.

Chicago Citizen's Association. 1889. *Annual Report of the Citizen's Association.*
———. 1888. *Annual Report of the Citizen's Association.*
Chicago City Council. 1914. *Report of the Gas Bureau of the Department of Public Service, City of Chicago, October 1, 1914.*
———. 1906. *Report of the Committee on Gas, Oil and Electric Light to the City Council of the City of Chicago, January 29, 1906.*
Chicago Examiner. Various issues and clippings files regarding Chicago gas matters. Chicago Historical Society.
Chicago Record-Herald. Various issues, 1905–1912.
Chicago Tribune. Various issues, 1870–1915.
Civic Federation of Chicago. 1897. *Chicago Gas Trust Bills: Another Attack on the People.* Pamphlet available at the Chicago Historical Society. No publisher.
Cleveland Leader and Herald. Various issues, 1889–1892 and 1909–1911.
Cleveland Plain Dealer. Various issues, 1889–1892 and 1909–1911.
Cleveland Press. Various issues, 1909–1911.
Coase, Ronald H. [1937] 1988. The Nature of the Firm. Reprinted in *The Firm, the Market, and the Law,* 33–56. Chicago: University of Chicago Press.
Commercial and Financial Chronicle. Various issues, 1880–1915.
Cowan, Geoffrey. 1933. *The People v. Clarence Darrow: The Bribery Trial of America's Greatest Laywer.* New York: Times Books, Random House, Inc.
Cowles, Alfred. 1939. *Common Stock Indexes.* Bloomington, IN: Principia Press.
Demsetz, Harold. 1968. Why Regulate Utilities? *Journal of Law and Economics* 11:55–65.
Denzau, Arthur T., and Michael C. Munger. 1986. Legislators and Interest Groups: How Unorganized Interests Get Represented. *American Political Science Review* 80:89–106.
Dimson, Elroy. 1979. Risk Measurement When Shares Are Subject to Infrequent Trading. *Journal of Financial Economics* 7:197–226.
Eggertsson, Thrain. 1990. *Economic Behavior and Institutions.* New York: Cambridge University Press.
Engineering News. Various issues, 1891–1892.
Fama, E. F., L. Fisher, M. Jensen, and R. Roll. 1969. The Adjustment of Stock Prices to New Information. *International Economic Review* 10:1–21.
Faye, C. Norman. 1909. *Plain Tales from Chicago.* Pamphlet reprinted from *Outlook,* March 6, 1909, 548–52. Available at the Chicago Historical Society.
Fiedler, George. 1973. *The Illinois Law Courts in Three Centuries, 1673–1973: A Documentary History.* Berwyn, IL: Physicians' Record Company.
Fogel, Robert. 1986. Nutrition and the Decline in Mortality since 1700. In *Long-Term Factors in American Economic Growth,* 439–527. Edited by Stanley Engerman and Robert Gallman. Chicago: University of Chicago Press.
Forestall, Walton. 1920. *A Manual of Gas Distribution.* Philadelphia: UGI Contracting.
Gabel, David. 1994. Competition in a Network Industry: The Telephone Industry, 1894–1910. *Journal of Economic History* 54:543–72.
Gely, Rafael, and Pablo T. Spiller. 1990. A Rational Choice Theory of Supreme

Court Statutory Decisions with Applications to the *State Farm* and *Grove City* Cases. *Journal of Law, Economics & Organization* 6:263–300.

Gilligan, Thomas W., and Keith Krehbiel. 1988. Complex Rules and Congressional Outcomes: An Event Study of Energy Tax Legislation. *Journal of Politics* 50:625–55.

Gilligan, Thomas W., William J. Marshall, and Barry W. Weingast. 1989. Regulation and the Theory of Legislative Choice: The Interstate Commerce Act of 1887. *Journal of Law and Economics* 32:35–61.

Ginger, Ray. 1958. *Altgeld's America: The Lincoln Ideal versus Changing Realities.* New York: Funk & Wagnalls.

Goldberg, Victor. 1976. Regulation and Administered Contracts. *Bell Journal of Economics* 7:426–52.

Gould, Jacob. 1946. *Output and Productivity in the Electric and Gas Utilities 1899–1942.* New York: National Bureau of Economic Research.

Grandy, Christopher. 1989. New Jersey Corporate Chartermongering, 1875–1929. *Journal of Economic History* 49:677–92.

Harrison, Carter. 1935. *Stormy Years: The Autobiography of Carter H. Harrison, Five Times Mayor of Chicago.* Indianapolis: The Bobbs-Merrill Company.

Holli, Melvin G. 1969. *Reform in Detroit: Hazen S. Pingree and Urban Politics.* New York: Oxford University Press.

Holmgren, Daniel F. 1964. Edward Webster Bemis and Municipal Reform. Unpublished Ph.D. dissertation. Western Reserve University.

Hovenkamp, Herbert. 1991. *Enterprise and American Law 1836–1937.* Cambridge, MA: Harvard University Press.

———. 1988. The Political Economy of Substantive Due Process. *Stanford Law Review* 40:404–60.

Hoyt, Homer. 1933. One Hundred Years of Land Values in Chicago. Published Ph.D. diss., University of Chicago. Private edition, distributed by University of Chicago Libraries.

Hunt, George. 1892. *Biennial Report of the Attorney General to the Governor of Illinois.* Springfield, IL: H. W. Rokker, State Printer and Binder.

———. 1890. *Biennial Report of the Attorney General to the Governor of Illinois.* Springfield, IL: H. W. Rokker, State Printer and Binder.

Ickes, Harold. 1943. *The Autobiography of a Curmudgeon.* New York: Reynal and Hitchcock.

Illinois Apportionment Handbook. 1911. Publisher and author unknown. Copy in author's possession received from the Illinois State Historical Society, Springfield, Illinois.

Illinois Bureau of Labor Statistics. 1897. *The Ninth Biennial Report of the Bureau of Labor Statistics of Illinois, Subject: Franchises and Taxation, 1896.* Springfield, IL: Phillips Brothers State Printers.

Illinois General Assembly. Illinois Legislative Public Utilities Commission. 1913. *Report of the Special Joint Committee to Investigate Public Utilities, April 17, 1913,* by John Daily, R. J. Barr, W. O. Potter, T. N. Gorman, W. P. Holaday, Chester W. Church, and William M. Scanlan. Springfield, IL.

Illinois General Assembly. The Special Committee on Public Utilities. 1917.

Majority and Minority Report of the Special Committee on Public Utilities of the Forty-Ninth General Assembly of the State of Illinois, January 20, 1917, by Medile McCormick, Thomas Gorman, Edward D. Shurtleff, Frederic R. De Young, Solomon Roderick, Frank R. Dalton, and George C. Hilton. Springfield, IL.

Jacobson, Charles. 1989. Same Game, Different Players: Problems in Urban Public Utility Regulation, 1850–1987. *Urban Studies* 26:13–31.

James, John A. 1983. Structural Change in American Manufacturing, 1850–1890. *Journal of Economic History* 43:433–59.

Jarrell, Gregg A. 1978. The Demand for State Regulation of the Electric Utility Industry. *Journal of Law and Economics* 21:269–96.

Journal of the House of the State of Illinois, various legislative sessions.

Journal of the Senate of the State of Illinois, various legislative sessions.

Kantowicz, Edward. 1995. Carter Harrison II: The Politics of Balance. In *The Mayors: The Chicago Political Tradition,* 16–32. Edited by Paul M. Green and Melvin G. Holli. Carbondale: Southern Illinois University Press.

———. 1975. *Polish-American Politics in Chicago, 1880–1940.* Chicago: University of Chicago Press.

Kneier, Charles M. 1927. *State Regulation of Public Utilities in Illinois.* University of Illinois Studies in the Social Sciences, ed. E. L. Bogart, J. A. Fairlie, and A. H. Lybyervol, vol. 14, no. 1. Urbana and Chicago: University of Illinois Press.

Kolko, Gabriel. 1963. *The Triumph of Conservatism: A Reinterpretation of American History, 1900–1916.* New York: Free Press.

Lebergott, Stanley. 1993. *Pursuing Happiness: American Consumers in the Twentieth Century.* Princeton: Princeton University Press.

———. 1976. *The American Economy: Income, Wealth and Want.* Princeton: Princeton University Press.

Libecap, Gary D. 1992. The Rise of the Chicago Packers and the Origins of Meat Inspection and Antitrust. *Economic Inquiry* 30:242–62.

McCaffrey, Lawrence J., Ellen Skerrett, Michael F. Fuchion, and Charles Fanning. 1987. *The Irish in Chicago.* Urbana and Chicago: University of Illinois Press.

McCarthy, Michael. 1974. Prelude to Armageddon: Charles E. Merriam and the Chicago Mayoral Election of 1911. *Journal of the Illinois State Historical Society* 67:505–18.

McCubbins, Matthew D., Roger G. Noll, and Barry R. Weingast. 1989. Structure and Process, Politics and Policy: Administrative Arrangements and the Political Control of Agencies. *Virginia Law Review* 75:431–82.

McCurdy, William E. 1925. The Power of a Public Utility to Fix its Rates and Charges in the Absence of Regulatory Legislation. *Harvard Law Review* 38:202–31.

McCusker, John. 1992. *How Much Is That in Real Money? A Historical Price Index for Use as a Deflator of Money Values in the Economy of the United States.* Worcester: American Antiquarian Society.

McDonald, Forrest. 1962. *Insull.* Chicago: University of Chicago Press.

———. 1958. Samuel Insull and the Movement for State Utility Regulatory Commissions. *Business History Review* 32:241–54.

———. 1957. *Let There Be Light: The Electric Utility Industry in Wisconsin, 1881–1955.* Madison, WI: American History Research Center.

McGee, John. 1958. Predatory Price Cutting: The Standard Oil (N.J.) Case. *Journal of Law and Economics* 1:137–69.

McMath, Robert C. 1975. *Populist Vanguard: A History of the Southern Farmers' Alliance.* Chapel Hill: University of North Carolina Press.

Merriam, Charles. 1929. *Chicago: A More Intimate View of Urban Politics.* New York: MacMillan Company.

Meyer, Robert A., and Hayne E. Leland. 1980. The Effectiveness of Price Regulation. *Review of Economics and Statistics* 62:555–71.

Miller, Geoffrey P. 1993. Comments on Priest. *Journal of Law and Economics* 36:325–30.

Miller, Zane L. 1968. *Boss Cox's Cincinnati: Urban Politics in the Progressive Era.* New York: Oxford University Press.

Minnesota Home-Rule League. 1914. *Regulation of Public Utilities in Wisconsin.* Minneapolis: Nygren Printing.

Moore, Thomas Gale. 1970. The Effectiveness of Regulation of Electric Utility Prices. *Southern Economic Journal* 36:365–81.

Morton, Richard Allen. 1990. Edward F. Dunne: Illinois' Most Progressive Governor. *Illinois Historical Journal* 83:13–30.

New York Times, various issues, 1883–1911.

Nisbet-Latta, M. 1907. *Hand-Book of American Gas Engineering Practice.* New York: D. Van Nostrand.

Nord, David Paul. 1979. *Newspapers and New Politics.* Ann Arbor: UMI Research Press.

North, Douglass C. 1990. *Institutions, Institutional Change, and Economic Performance.* New York: Cambridge University Press.

———. 1981. *Structure and Change in Economic History.* New York: W. W. Norton.

Olson, Mancur. 1971. *The Logic of Collective Action.* Cambridge: Cambridge University Press.

Opinions of the Corporation Counsel and Assistants, From January 1, 1913 to October 5, 1914.

Palmer, John M. 1899. *The Bench and Bar of Illinois, Historical and Reminiscent, Volume I.* Chicago: Lewis Publishing.

Passer, Harold C. 1953. *The Electrical Manufacturers, 1875–1900.* Cambridge: Harvard University Press.

Pegram, Thomas R. 1992. *Partisans and Progressives: Private Interest and Public Policy in Illinois, 1870–1922.* Urbana and Chicago: University of Illinois Press.

Peoples Gas Light and Coke Company, Annual Reports, 1897–1924.

Peoples Gas Light and Coke Company. 1900. *Statement of the Peoples Gas Light and Coke Company to Its Consumers.* Pamphlet found at the Chicago Historical Society. No publisher.

Pierce, Bessie Louise. 1957. *A History of Chicago,* vols. 1–3. New York: A. A. Knopf.

Pierce, P. S. 1982. *The Dow Jones Averages, 1885–1980.* Homewood, IL: Dow Jones-Irwin.

Platt, Harold L. 1991. *The Electric City: Energy and the Growth of the Chicago Area, 1880–1930.* Chicago: University of Chicago Press.

Pond, Oscar Lewis. [1906] 1968. *Municipal Control of Public Utilities: A Study of the Attitude of Our Courts toward an Increase of the Sphere of Municipal Activity.* Reprint, New York: AMS Press.

Posner, Richard. 1994. What Do Judges and Justices Maximize? The Same Thing Everybody Else Does. *Supreme Court Economic Review* 3:1–41.

Pratt, John C. 1885. *Present State of the Gas Interest* (paper presented at the meetings of the American Gas Association, Cincinnati, OH, October 21, 1885). Boston: Gunn Curtis Company.

Priest, George L. 1993. The Origins of Utility Regulation and the "Theories of Regulation Debate." *Journal of Law and Economics* 36:289–324.

Quincy Daily Herald. Various issues, 1913.

Rasmussen, Eric. 1994. Judicial Legitimacy as a Repeated Game. *Journal of Law, Economics and Organization* 10:63–83.

Rice, Wallace. 1925. *75 Years of Gas Service in the City of Chicago.* Chicago: Peoples Gas Light and Coke Company.

Richards, William. 1877. *A Practical Treatise on the Manufacture and Distribution of Coal Gas.* London: E. and F. N. Spon.

Roberts, Sidney I. 1960. The Municipal Voters' League and Chicago's Boodlers. *The Journal of the Illinois State Historical Society* 53:117–48.

Rose, Mark H. 1995. *Cities of Light and Heat: Domesticating Gas and Electricity in Urban America.* University Park: Pennsylvania State University Press.

Rutten, Andrew. 1991. The Supreme Court and the Search for an Economic Constitution, 1870–1990. Unpublished Ph.D. diss., Washington University, St. Louis, MO.

Shelton, F. 1889. Illuminating Water Gas—Past and Present. Paper presented at proceedings of the American Gas Light Association.

Shepsle, Kenneth A. 1992. Bureaucratic Drift, Coalitional Drift, and Time Consistency: A Comment on Macey. *Journal of Law, Economics and Organization* 8:111–18.

Shepsle, Kenneth A., and Barry W. Weingast. 1987. The Institutional Foundations of Committee Power. *American Political Science Review* 81:85–104.

Smith, Henry Ezmond. 1926. Organization and Administrative Procedures of the Peoples Gas Light and Coke Company. Unpublished Ph.D. diss., University of Chicago.

Springfield Illinois State Register. Various issues, 1913.

Stigler, George J. 1985. The Origins of the Sherman Act. *Journal of Legal Studies,* 14:1–11.

Stigler, George J., and Claire Friedland. 1962. What Can Regulators Regulate? The Case of Electricity. *Journal of Law and Economics* 5:1–16.

Stotz, Louis P., and Alexander Jamison. 1938. *History of the Gas Industry.* New York: Stettiner Brothers.

Tarr, Joel. 1971. *A Study in Boss Politics: William Lorimer of Chicago.* Urbana: University of Illinois Press.

———. 1966. John R. Walsh of Chicago: A Case Study in Banking and Politics, 1881–1905. *Business History Review* 40:451–66.

Tate, James H. 1985. *Keeper of the Flame: The Story of the Atlanta Gas Light Company, 1856–1985.* Atlanta: Atlanta Gas Light Company.

Tenant, Richard B. 1950. *The American Cigarette Industry: A Study in Economic Analysis and Public Policy.* New Haven: Yale University Press.

Thelen, David. 1972. *The New Citizenship: Origins of Progressivism in Wisconsin, 1885–1900.* Columbia: University of Missouri Press.

Tierney, Kevin. 1979. *Darrow: A Biography.* New York: Thomas Y. Crowell.

Troesken, Werner. 1994. Senator Sherman, Standard Oil and the Battle for Antitrust. Unpublished paper, Department of History, University of Pittsburgh.

United Gas Improvement Company. 1911. *Carbureted Water Gas.* Philadelphia: Edward Stern.

United States Department of Commerce, Bureau of the Census. 1975. *Historical Statistics of the United States, Colonial Times to 1970.* Washington, DC: Government Printing Office.

United States Department of the Interior, Census Office. 1902. *Twelfth Census of the United States, Taken in the Year 1900. Manufacturers, Part IV.* Washington, DC: Government Printing Office.

———. 1895. *Report on Manufacturing Industries in the United States at the Eleventh Census: 1890. Part II. Statistics of the Cities.* Washington, DC: Government Printing Office.

———. 1895. *Report on Manufacturing Industries in the United States at the Eleventh Census: 1890. Part III. Selected Industries.* Washington, DC: Government Printing Office.

———. 1894. *Compendium of the Eleventh Census: 1890. Part II: Vital and Social Statistics; Educational and Church.* Washington, DC: Government Printing Office.

Van Sinderen, Lindsley. 1906. *Rate Regulation of Gas and Electric Lighting.* New York: The Banks Law Publishing Company.

Van Tassel, David D., and John J. Grabowski. 1987. *Encyclopedia of Cleveland History.* Bloomington: Indiana University Press.

Weber, George Welsh. 1919. *Political History of Chicago's Gas Question.* Sixteen-page pamphlet at Chicago Historical Society. No publisher.

Weingast, Barry W., and William Marshall. 1988. The Industrial Organization of Congress; or, Why Legislatures, Like Firms, Are Not Organized as Markets. *Journal of Political Economy* 96:132–63.

Wendt, Lloyd, and Herman Kogan. 1943. *Lords of the Levee: The Story of Bathhouse John and Hinky Dink.* Indianapolis: Bobbs-Merrill.

Wilcox, Delos F. 1910. *Municipal Franchises: A Description of the Terms and Con-*

ditions upon which Private Corporations Enjoy Special Privileges in the Streets of American Cities. Vol. 1. New York: McGraw Hill.

Williamson, Oliver. 1985. *The Economic Institutions of Capitalism.* New York: Free Press.

Wood, Edward S. 1877. *Illuminating Gas in Its Relation to Health.* Pamphlet reprinted from vol. 3, Public Health Papers of the American Public Health Association. Cambridge, MA: Riverside Press.

Index